*All souls do not easily recall the
things of the other world. Few are they who
keep an adequate remembrance of them.*

- Plato

Front cover: Lichfield Abbey

STAFFORDSHIRE:
its magic & mystery

Doug Pickford

Published by Sigma Leisure - an imprint of
Sigma Press, 1 South Oak Lane, Wilmslow, Cheshire SK9 6AR, England.

British Library Cataloguing in Publication Data
A CIP record for this book is available from the British Library.

ISBN: 1-85058-426-5

Typesetting and Design by: Sigma Press, Wilmslow, Cheshire.

Cover design : The Agency, Wilmslow

Printed by: Manchester Free Press

Dedication and Acknowledgments:

This book is dedicated to our children and grandchildren.

Many have helped in ways large and small with this work. Thanks go from my dear wife Hilary and myself to Val Pownall for inputting; and to countless others who have assisted with ideas and with practical and spiritual assistance, including Maurice Winnell. Appreciation and acknowledgement for access to files and for permission to quote from them goes to the *Congleton Chronicle* and the *Evening Sentinel*. If I have not mentioned you, please accept my apologies - my mind is too full.

Contents

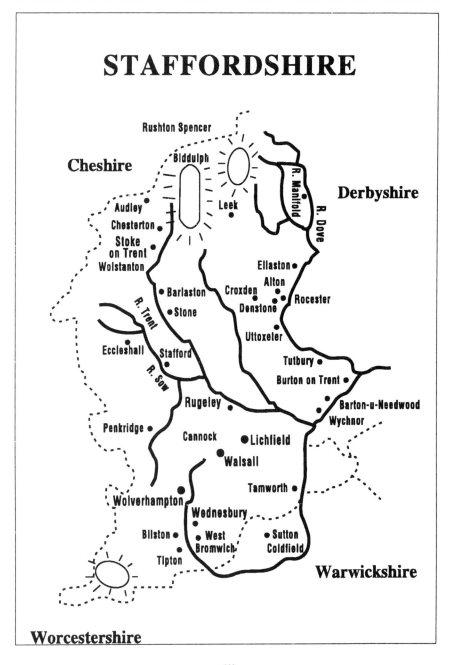

STAFFORDSHIRE

1

The Hidden County

Many years ago I had an aunt who, I remember, told me that Staffordshire was "the Hidden County". She had been entertaining some second cousins, once removed, for tea (they had called on her, unannounced, and had been made very welcome) and were, I think, in these parts for a brief holiday. They had asked where there was to go and what there was to see in Staffordshire. "There isn't much to do here, is there?" one of them said.

I don't remember her reply to him but I do remember the wry smile that came over her. Anyway, whatever transpired seemed to please the distant relations and away they went.

"There isn't much to do auntie," I said to her afterwards. "He was right."

It was then that I remember her telling me that this is the Hidden County.

"Who's it hiding from?"

"From people who don't look for it" she answered. And that was it. End of conversation.

I often wondered about what she had said; I was a mere lad and her enigmatic answer was lost on me for many a year. Of course I now know what she meant but I had to ponder; I had to discover and I had to search for that discovery.

About the same time, I read a book from the school library. It was by Mark Hughes who had been Headmaster of Christ Church Schools in Stone. There was a piece within its pages that stayed with me, just like auntie's wry smile and her mysterious reply to

1

her relative. It was part of his description of this County that will be forever etched in my mind. He had written of this Shire that ... "the voice of the past cries out to us in every rock and tree, hill and valley, cave and moor ... nor are there wanting silent records of the men and women who dwelt here in those bygone times; man, too, has left his footprints in the sands of time."

The first dawning of realisation began. Later, as I approached manhood I was allowed to share secrets that had been in my family for generations and it was then I knew for certain what was Hidden and, indeed, what was "Magical and Mysterious" about Staffordshire. The clues are all around, we just have to search for them with our eyes wide open and our blinkers discarded and after we have discovered the clues we can be led on to the answers.

Staffordshire can be all things to anyone. On the surface it can be the industrialised Black Country to the south or the wild and windswept Bleak Country to the north. But scratch just underneath that surface and the veneer will shine. The Black Country may now suffer from a heritage of greedy industry but only a few hundred years ago it was alive with the ways of old, it was a rural spot where the Earth was the goddess and the Heart of England beat with pride and vigour. And of course this is still the case. Yes, there is still a hangover from the intoxicated Industrial Revolution but there is a pride within its people, there is still an intense appreciation of the place and there is a remembrance of the Old Ways.

This is the Hidden County.

England in Miniature

To the north within the Moorlands we have one of the most beautiful and unspoilt areas anyone could possibly imagine. An unmistakable pride beats strongly within the breasts of Moorland men and women and the mysterious and unrecognised is still very much a part of these inhabitants.

The Heartland, where the Green Man and Robin Goodfellow still roam (if you search for them) is cloaked in an atmosphere of the hauntingly beautiful. Nature is still the driving force here and the people respect it.

One son of Staffordshire was the novelist Arnold Bennett who coined the phrase "The Five Towns" for the Potteries. He describes this County in one of his books, "The Old Wives' Tale". In it he tells of where two of the book's characters are living within the Potteries and he writes of Staffordshire itself:

"They were established almost precisely on the fifty third parallel of latitude. A little way to the north of them, in the creases of a hill famous for its religious orgies, rose the River Trent, the calm and characteristic stream of middle England. Somewhat further northwards, in the near neighbourhood of the highest public house in the realm, rose two lesser rivers, the Dane and the Dove, which, quarrelling in early infancy, turned their backs on each other, and, the one by favour of the Weaver and the other by favour of the Trent, watered between them the whole width of England, and poured themselves respectively into the Irish Sea and the German Ocean. What a county of modest, unnoticed rivers! What a natural, simple county, content to fix its boundaries by these tortuous island brooks, with their comfortable names – Trent, Mease, Dove, Tern, Dane, Mees, Stour, Tame and even hasty Severn! Not that the Severn is suitable to the County! In the county excess is deprecated. The county is happy in not exciting remark. It is content that Shropshire should possess that swollen bump, the Wrekin, and that the exaggerated wilderness of the Peak should lie over its border. It does not desire to be a pancake like Cheshire. It has everything that England has, including thirty miles of Watling Street; and England can show nothing more beautiful and nothing uglier than the works of nature and the works of man to be seen within the limits of the county. It is England in miniature, lost in the midst of England, unsung by searchers after the extreme; perhaps occasionally sore at this neglect, but how proud in the instinctive cognizance of its representative features and traits!"

Magic and Mystery

This is a land of contrasts. It is also a land of magic and mystery and is hauntingly beautiful, elegant and rugged. It is also a Shire that has had more than its fair share of exploitation. Yet it retains traditions that are as old as time, it hangs on to its beauty and it will never let go of its knowledge of the earth. Its people are aware of its powerful hold on them and they are aware of much that has gone before. It is a land of opposites and it is a land of togetherness. There is much this Shire can still give and there is much it still wants to give. There is a great deal to explore and a great deal of exploring to be done.

The northernmost parts are high and mighty and beautiful moorlands containing the southernmost tip of the Pennine Chain. To some they may seem bleak but to others they are vital and alive. They are full of life (and lives) now gone. There are countless valleys running through and there are roads criss-crossing but, not so very long ago, the north was said to be an impassable barrier and this barrier divided the north dwellers with the south dwellers. There was dense woodland, mainly that of the Forest of Lyme dividing Staffordshire and Cheshire and also dividing North Staffs with the heartland and southlands of the County. But the centre of the Shire had woodland as well and its entire mass spread eastward, to Nottingham and beyond. These thickly wooded lands were haunted, it was said, by the spirits of the forest ... Puck, Robin Goodfellow and the Hooded Man – Robin – and the horned deity still remembered at Abbotts Bromley.

To the West there is also Shropshire but no natural boundary here, only a barrier of traditions and memory. To the south of these wild and wonderful moorlands there is the fertile and the broad valley of the Trent and this majestic river with its tributaries the Dove and the Tame, forms the eastern borders.

And then, to the south, is the ancient and haunting area known as Cannock Chase, the scene of the royal hunts and the scene of the Wild Hunts of legend and tradition. This land of the hunt and the chase is still, in small parts, wooded. Much of Staffordshire south of the Trent was once one huge forested land making up the royal forests of Cannock and Kinver along with Needwood Forest. This, too, is a land of tradition where the ghosts of the past still haunt and where Robin of the Hood and his mystical bride still stroll hand in hand. Now, most of the trees have been destroyed, countless thousands axed during the Middle Ages for the smelting of ironstone.

Long before the Romans used the already existing long highways through here, Staffordshire was occupied and venerated by people who worshipped the Earth in the form of the Great Goddess the Earth Mother. In the north this goddess, Brigit, is still remembered at The Bridestones; the mighty god Woden lives on at Wednesbury and the Fires of Baal.

This is the land that was home to the White and Blue robed wise men of Celtic race, the Druids and the Ovates, and it is the land that possesses what is probably the finest example of a Druid's Sacred Grove in the entire country ... still intact because of the knowledge retained by Staffordshire people and in the most unlikely of spots close by the Potteries. This is a land of so many contrasts; contrasts of history, geography and people – but never a contrast of tradition and reverence for that which has gone before.

The Old Knowledge

In my previous books based on East Cheshire, the Staffordshire Moorlands and the Peak District, I have endeavoured to show that much that has been forgotten is still with us. I have tried to show that the Spirit of the Place still haunts; I have endeavoured to explain that much of the Knowledge of the Ancients may have been suppressed but is still lurking in the visions and thoughts of many and I have done my best to describe the reasons why so much is what it is today. We can thank our forefathers for possessing the knowledge that is still helping us.

Here in Staffordshire there are still stones and waters that have the power to heal, there are still people with the ability to appreciate the Lie of the Land and there are still traditions, myths and legends that are very much alive. And there are still mysteries to be solved.

Please join me on a magical mystery tour of this great Shire where we shall meet dragons and witches, ghosts and fairies as well as knights of old and warriors bold ... where we shall meet ourselves and where we shall find Staffordshire.

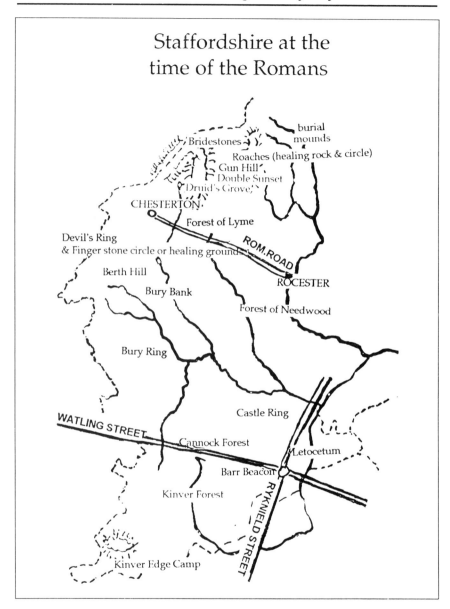

Staffordshire at the time of the Romans

burial mounds

Bridestones

Roaches (healing rock & circle)

Gun Hill,
Double Sunset
Druid's Grove,

CHESTERTON

Forest of Lyme

Devil's Ring
& Finger stone circle or healing ground

ROM.ROAD

Berth Hill

ROCESTER

Bury Bank

Forest of Needwood

Bury Ring

Castle Ring

WATLING STREET

Cannock Forest

Letocetum

Barr Beacon

Kinver Forest

RYKNIELD STREET

Kinver Edge Camp

Showing the major roads used by the Romans (they were probably constructed before the Roman occupation, however) and the main religious sites existing then.

6

2

STONES OF STAFFORDSHIRE

A County-wide search

Enigmatic stone circles are plentiful in neighbouring Derbyshire and to the West across the Dyke built by Staffordshire's former overlord Offa; but within our own County these stones of time are less obvious. Monoliths erected to great leaders are plentiful, though, and their usual abode is in a churchyard or in the centre of a town.

Not that there haven't been plenty of circles in the past but industry, housing and agriculture have all done their best to ensure that they have been done away with. Add to that the puritan zeal of some people who, in the past, have decided that the pagan aspects of our predecessors should be destroyed and it becomes all too clear that these monuments to the earth, moon, sun and stars didn't stand a chance.

It is easy to visualise that many of our churches were built on sites venerated by pre-Christians and perhaps some of these, on high hills, were where the circles of stones tapped into the earth energies. When the early Christians toppled these stone acupuncture "needles", they did not destroy the energy they were tapping into for they erected stones of their own and when they built their own structures to their own God (and Goddess, the Virgin Mary) they, albeit unwittingly, tapped into the earth energies themselves. Even today, some people are able to channel this energy for their own good. How many people come away from a Church service feeling uplifted both spiritually and physically? Some of this can be thanks to the preacher, but some can also be thanks to the energy still contained at the site, I am certain.

Today, the best places to search for these stones are the areas of hill and moorland and so, in the main, we must look to the north of our Shire. But there are other places as well, as we shall discover. For not only should we look to the stones, we should also look to the burial mounds – mounds usually containing a Chieftain or a Holy Man. These people were usually buried on top of the hills and covered with mounds of earth or heaps of stones. These barrows or lowes were, more often than not, on sites where there was one strong earth energy line at the very least and, most probably, two or more converging. A number of eminent Victorian gentlemen had a hobby or pastime of uncovering these mounds and whether or not we should "thank" them I do not care to say. They certainly unearthed the urns and the arrowheads and the necklaces of semi-precious stones buried with the dead to see them through their journey to the after-life (the smaller urns often contained ale or other alcoholic brew and the larger contained the burned or calcified bones of the deceased) and, no doubt, they had food with them as well for their journey but this would have rotted within weeks. One of the chief diggers into the past was a Mr Carrington, the schoolmaster at Wetton, between the years 1846 and 1850. Around the area where he taught, between the River Manifold and the River Dove, these burial mounds are more plentiful than anywhere else in Staffordshire. Another digger who unearthed countless sites was named Bateman.

The Bridestones

Undoubtedly one of the finest examples of Stones once in this County is the group known as The Bridestones. Staffordshire can only just lay claims to these because the Cheshire border lies here also; and a group of stones that once made up part of the circle now lie in a garden just over the county border. The stones have straddled the borders for many centuries, and both counties can claim them.

So what do we know of these enigmatic stones? A number of people, and I count myself among them, believe that the Bridestones were once as important, if not more important, than

Stonehenge itself. Unfortunately what was once a massive structure has been destroyed over the centuries; the chief culprits being the early road makers who pillaged the stones to use on the nearby turnpike road that goes to Congleton. In 1764 it is recorded that several hundred loads of stones were taken away from the site for making the road. This used to be the road taken by the Earls of Chester to their spiritual home at Dieulacres Abbey just north of Leek, and is still known as The Earlsway. It was also the road used by the monks to herd the sheep to the Cheshire markets and to bring in salt from the Cheshire Wyches. The Bridestones is one of the few long barrows found in Britain with a paved forecourt and the name comes from St Bride, the Christianised form of a pagan name "Brigit" the fertility goddess of the Brigantes.

How sad that our ancestors decided the hard-core of a road should be more important than this monument to a goddess of old.

Today, there is little left to show the splendour that was. Two uprights still look westwards over the Cheshire plain and towards the home of the builders of this monument – the people of Ireland. When they came over to the mainland in their small boats, most probably sailing up the River Dee, they then walked or rode over the flat plain and the first high land they came to – and the first high land with powerful earth energies – was where they erected their temple to their goddess.

So just what is there today? The sides and the ends of the Bridestones still intact are formed of unhewn stones with a single rock, nine and a half feet (almost three metres) high at the head. The whole of this remaining part appears to have formed a large chest some 18 feet long (five and a half metres) and 11 feet wide (about three and a half metres). This was the burial chamber and this is where my dowsing rods show there to be a very powerful earth energy line. Did the Ancients place their dead there in the hope of re-birth from this energy, I wonder? At certain times of the year, most probably the summer and spring equinoxes, this energy would have increased. I know of someone who received an electric shock when he touched the stone, the force being strong enough to knock him to the ground. The energy is still there, but not all of us know how to tap in to it.

The Bridestones. There are still local stories told in Staffordshire that, up until this century, couples would come to these stones to be "married". Is this a throw-back to the fertility cult, of which the deity Brigit was head? Many people used to be married "over the brush" in days gone by, and for a time this was their 'church'. It straddles the Staffordshire border and its area was very much of the County – and it still is.

I have looked into this site in great detail in a previous book on East Cheshire and the Moorlands and mentioned therein the lane that goes around this site, known as Dial Lane. This refers to the clockwise direction taken by people who perambulated around an ancient site, usually a Holy site. Dial is the natural way to go. The opposite is widdershins – against the sun. And that is un-natural.

The Devil's Ring and Finger

Near to Mucklestone just south west of Newcastle under Lyme, there is the Devil's Ring and Finger.

Other stones are associated with the Devil and this is because anything that was not Christian must, in the eyes of our devout ancestors, have been evil; therefore of the Devil. In the village of

10

Rushton Spencer, for instance, north of Leek, there is a church dedicated to St Laurence. It stands just a little way off the Earlsway that travels past the Bridestones. It is on a high hillock and can often be seen jutting out of the mist when a blanket of fog or mist cloaks the valley below in which nestles the village of Rushton. It is said that when the Cistercian monks came to nearby Dieulacres Abbey they founded a chapel at this site and pushed a stone or boulder down the southerly slope of the hill. This stone was called Satan's Stone and had markings on it which were referred to as the devil's apron strings. The story goes that each night the devil picked up the stone in his apron and carried it back up the hill, hence the marks from his apron strings. And each day the monks would roll it down the hill again. Certainly this is not the only place to have such a story told. Perhaps the local people did take the stone back to its original site because it had been there for a very specific purpose. Whether or not, there is no doubt whatsoever that the site of this church had religious significance, albeit pagan, before the Cistercians decided to Christianise it.

This stone could be seen in the fields below the church until, I am told, the early 1960s, when for agricultural purposes it had to, unfortunately, be removed. I was never able to visit the stone myself and only heard the tale after it had gone, but I have been told by a number of people that one of the men who were removing it – with a small piece of dynamite for a quick job – had some of his fingers blown off. I have not been able to verify this so do not know if it is modern-day folklore or not.

The Roaches

Close by this spot, and towering above the site of the Cistercian Abbey of Dieulacres, are the magnificent rocks known as The Roaches. I would be guilty of unnecessary repetition if I was to go into the magical and the mysterious aspects of these wonderful rocky outcrops for my previous two works on the supernatural and the paranormal have both made lengthy reference to the healing rocks and the sacrificial stones within this land of the High Rocks, as I have termed it. But what I have not mentioned before is a stone circle close by a healing rock and there is a very good reason for

11

that – this circle had not been discovered at the time of my writing the previous works.

Take the road out of Leek towards Buxton and at the first signpost for Upperhulme (wrongly shown as Upper Hulme) turn left, travel past the cottages by the ford and through the site of the industrial works. The road then bears right and takes the traveller along and beneath Hen Cloud and the high rocks and there are parking bays kindly supplied by the Peak Park. There was, the last time I went there, a van selling fish and chips and the smell – delightful as it was – was completely and utterly out of place (or should it be plaice?). I got it in my mind that I would complain and, low and behold, I read in the local paper, the Leek Post, the same week that I was not the only one who thought it not befitting the grandeur of the place and it would be removed. With the best will in the world towards the gentleman who was trying to make a living from his travelling take-away, I hope he finds a more lucrative spot than this and I hope the travellers in search of the healing rock and the stone circle are not troubled by any more smells of civilisation. There are still people who make a pilgrimage to this rock, known as the Bawd Stone, to be healed and I am told that as a result of my previous book in which I make mention of this healing stone there has been a marked increase in pilgrims.

A few yards, or metres, south of this rock there is a mound of earth some forty or so feet in diameter. It is overgrown with bilberry bushes and these bushes have done their best to hide a stone circle.

In the winter of 1993 I and a good friend, Maurice Winnell, who is something of an amateur archaeologist, visited the Bawd Stone for the umpteenth time to get some line-ups with the compass points and the sighting points for the solstices, not to mention to use the dowsing rods to find if there are any earth energy lines travelling through. Sure enough there are these energy lines – I would have been very surprised if there were not any because of the healing properties of this stone – and sure enough the stone lined up with the hills to the east which gave a clear indication of the spring equinox. Immediately to the south there stands the mighty Hen Cloud and there we saw an obviously man-made cleft within the outline of the rocks and this, from the Bawd Stone, proved to be exactly on the summer solstice.

Between the Bawd Stone and the Hen Cloud rocks we discovered the stone circle.

The circle of stones on the Roaches, due south of the Bawdstone.

The word circle is not the right description because it is more of an oval shape than anything and the rocks that are remaining number about forty in all, the tallest being some four feet or so in height.

And we also found that there was an inner circle (or oval) as well. It was impossible to uncover the circle because that would have meant disturbing the ground and disturbing the bilberry bushes and this we were loath to do. Perhaps some day a University or Museum somewhere will be able to get permission from the Peak Park to have a better look at this site but until then I would appeal to everyone to treat it with tender loving care. Look by all means but please don't touch. Fortunately it stands by the well-defined path that leads over the backbone of the Roaches to Hen Cloud so it can be viewed without straying from the rights of way (and I rather suspect that some of the stones have at one point been used

13

in the construction of this path, probably when the Princess of Teck was entertained to a picnic on the rocks behind Rock Hall by the then owners of the land, the Brocklehursts). My great grandfather, William, had the honour of carving a stone seat from a rock for the royal visitor (he was a stone mason) and this stone seat and a plaque commemorating the visit can be seen to this day close by where the rock-climbers' shelter now stands.

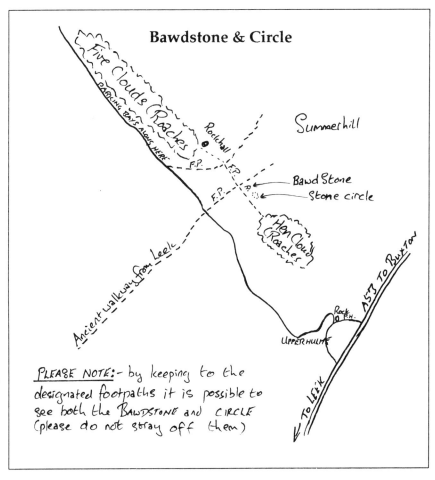

It is easy to view the Bawd Stone and circle from the major footpath south to Hen Cloud. Please keep to the footpath.

There have been other stone circles, as I have said, now with churches built over the sites. And there have been a number of hill forts within this county. The best known of these today are Bury Ring near Stafford, Bury Bank near Stone (of which more later) Berth Hill near Maer, Kinver Edge Camp, Castle Ring and the fort on Bosley Cloud straddling the borderline of Staffordshire and Cheshire. These constructions were almost certainly made for the purpose of defence and, like the stone circles, are all on high ground with wide views all the way around. In every instance there is a supply of water nearby and are all of a size to accommodate a good number of people, plus it is assumed, the livestock as well. They all had earthworks of stone and earth and clay to a height of some six feet (two metres) or so and would have had sharp stakes on top of these and, according to Stone headmaster Mark Hughes, they were all connected "by grass tracks".

Burial Mounds

There is also Castle Ring, close to Burton on Trent. This has been called the finest British Camp that still remains and is perched so high that it has been possible to see nine counties from it. Roughly circular, there are two ditches surrounding the camp and across it is a track running from north east to south west which gave narrow openings into the fortification. Unfortunately, mining subsidence has caused much damage. It is about 270 metres across.

A list of Staffordshire burial mounds was compiled in 1817 by an often-quoted man named Pitt. He wrote that there was a large one, but in 1817 just a ruck of stones, at Hints, close to Watling Street and another at Calf Heath. There were two at Kingswinford, one at Great Saredon, two on Golwich Common, another at Mathfield, two around Okeover, no less than three on Morridge near Leek, three on the Weaver Hills and named as Queen Low, Gallows Knoll and Astlow Cross. He said that Lows were also to be found at Ribden, Reeden and the Cauldon Hills (where quarrying at the aptly named Cauldon Lowe has destroyed them) and on Wombourne Common. Near to Warslow, that name itself implying a burial place, there used to be Cocklow and this was excavated in

1852 by Thomas Bateman. In the year 1905 it was destroyed to make way for a new road but thankfully a Leek vicar named the Rev. W. Beresford was able to record that the height was some 18 feet and its diameter was some fifty yards. A burial urn was dug up and a vase was accidentally broken but this showed that it contained the bones of a child and some of them had been hacked at or cut. A crudely carved sandstone heart was also found there. Perhaps this child had been a sacrifice, but more likely this child died in battle or was attacked in some way or another. Undoubtedly it was the son or daughter of a high-ranking person. There is still a legend at Warslow that the ghost of a young boy can be seen walking the road where the burial site was disturbed. Perhaps the boy is looking for his earthly place of rest ... who knows? There was also a Cock Lowe at Leek, which was destroyed to build housing upon – where Westwood Road and Spring Gardens now stand.

On Hen Cloud is a pool called Doxey Pool. Here, it is said, there lurks a mermaid ... just like the one seen at the Mermaid's Pool over at Morridge. An "evil looking hag" has also been reported as having been seen in its waters.

The Bury

The 1817 list says there are others on the hills near Warslow and one at Onecote near to Leek. Near to Wednesfield, named after the god Woden, there are three sites: Stowman Low, North Lowfield and South Lowfield and at nearby Bushbury is another. At Cannock Chase there were many recorded. Near to Milford is a cup-shaped barrow known as The Bury in which there were found three different lots of human bones, all burned. There is a local tradition here that this is the resting place of three chieftains and, as only the hierarchy were buried in these places, it is quite possibly correct. Local tradition counts for a lot in my view, for although distorted, perhaps, by word of mouth over the centuries, there is usually an element of truth to be found. Bury Bank is also said to be the burial place of a giant – perhaps not a giant as we would think of one (as in the tale of Jack and the Beanstalk) more probably a giant among men – a warrior leader.

What an amazing place is Bury Bank. There is not much to see in this day and age, hardly surprising when you consider how long it is that time has ravaged the spot. But the magic remains and so does the mystery.

Hilary, my son Charles (who, like me, is a dowser) and I paid a visit to this spot one February morning. Parking our car on the back road to Tittensor, we took the track known locally as the Nuns' Walk, so named because a house across the road from Bury Bank Farm was once a Nunnery and the occupants of the house took this way to Tittensor Church, it is said. There is also the local tradition that a tunnel connected this Nunnery to Tittensor Church; unlikely but it sounded very familiar. Several "secret tunnels" we have investigated have turned out to be ley lines or earth energy lines and this was no exception. Always believe that local tradition has a foundation in fact.

The Chase

The walk across The Chase, through the man-made forest where wild deer still roam, was a delight. Here there still is earth magic. We followed the ancient route past the burial mound known as

Saxon's Low to our left. What secrets could this mound tell, I wonder? The answer must be many, but it has no intention of divulging any. And I rather suspect that the Saxon period is not the correct dating; far earlier, I think. After the pleasant stroll we came to Bury Bank Farm to what must be the end of the journey. The occupants bade us welcome but the earthworks over the barbed wire fence are not on their land and there are no public rights of way to it. But they did allow us to get as near as possible, for which I must thank them. From the outside looking in it was still possible to capture the majesty of the place. Trees planted a good few years ago should not have been allowed, I think, because their roots must have disturbed the spot. However, much of the earthwork can still be seen and there is much to be viewed but permission must be sought. I cannot emphasise this enough. This fort, castle or, indeed, palace, is on a spot that overlooks the Trent and there has been much erosion over the years, but it is still possible to see ramparts and ditches.

Saxon's Lowe. What secrets does it hold?

There was much psychic energy around the spot that morning, and Hilary saw two figures clearly in psychic vision, one male and leading a fine brown stallion and the other female, with long gold hair, seated on the horse. Two time scales crossed – ours and theirs – and it was clear that this woman was visiting the spot for the first time, just as we were doing. But she was being led there by her new husband, many hundreds of years in time difference. ·

Barrow Cop Hill

Mention must also be made of Barrow Cop Hill where, again, three Kings are said to be buried and, again, this is most probably correct if we look upon the Kings as being chieftains of a clan or tribe.

Near to Brownhills it is recorded that Catshill, formerly Cutteslowe (the burial mound of Cutha) contains the remains of the warrior brother of Ceawlin, the conqueror of Mercia and founder of Wednesbury ... and a worshipper of Woden. However, the word "Cat" in this context also implies the site of an ancient battle. There is Cat Tor on the hills of North Staffordshire which is reputed to have this connotation.

There are many more in this ancient Shire of ours, too many to mention; there are many that have gone under the plough and there are some that have not yet been identified. Many were saved because of the reverence shown for them by our predecessors. It was often considered unlucky to plough up an ancient burial site (thank goodness) and it was sometimes said that these were fairy hills, where the little people were said to live and be buried. Any flint arrowheads that were unearthed were said to be fairy spears. For a more in-depth look at this aspect I would refer you to the chapter on the Fairy Folk of Biddulph Moor.

And finally, at Barlaston a grave was found on the top of a 500 foot high hill about two miles away from the hill fort or palace known as Bury Bank. The grave, it is said, was cut into rock made of sandstone and lay in line with the poles, north and south. There was no trace of the skeleton (perhaps animals had had it, or then again perhaps some human "animals" had had it) but in the grave itself was an iron sword nearly a metre long, a dagger, and a bowl made from bronze. I know of a psychic medium who has visited this place and has seen the warrior chieftain who was buried there. His soul, she says, is in torment and he needs releasing from this torment. That she is endeavouring to do. I wish her well.

Oh, and his name sounded to her like Wolf something or other. I would here refer you to the following piece about Stone and the warrior princes ... called Wulfad and Rufin ...

Riddle of Stone

We could not possibly discuss the stones of Staffordshire without a look at a township named after one – Stone itself. The traditional reason for it being so named will be looked at but I have to say here and now that I disagree with the tale, and I hope to convince you just why I do.

Stone itself is a pleasant town with pleasant people living in it. Unfortunately, at the time of writing, it is a town laid siege by the motor vehicle. My most recent visit proved to be most enjoyable with the shops, hostelries and people all being most welcoming, but the heavy lorries bounding and banging along the main street were something I, and I'm sure the people of Stone, could do without. I believe a by-pass is on the way, thank goodness.

However, our search for the stone begins, thankfully, many hundreds of years before the infernal combustion engine and it also begins some two miles or so out of Stone at an ancient hill fortress already mentioned, by the name of Bury Bank. It is here, tradition says, that Wulfere, King of Mercia, had a fortified palace and the area was known as Wulferecester or Wulfere's town. He was a pagan, just like his father, Penda (so we are told) and he wished to marry a princess from the royal house of Kent who was named Ermendilda. Her family refused to let him marry her because he worshipped the earth gods and she was Christian but he agreed to be converted to Christianity, married, and quickly reverted back to his old ways. They had three children, boys named Wulfad and Rufin and a daughter named Werburga, over whose grave rose the cathedral of Chester. It is said that Wulfere reverted to paganism after being "shaken by incessant wars" and who knows, this may be correct, and he allowed his daughter to be brought up a Christian but the boys – both warrior princes – were "heathens".

20

The story goes that Wulfad was hunting on horseback in a forest and followed a large hart who disappeared near to a cave. In that cave, which I think was at the place where Walton, near Stone, now is, there was a hermit who turned out to be no less a personage than Chad, later Saint Chad, the bringer of Christianity to these parts. His name lives on at Lichfield (St Chad's Church) where the mighty Christian diocese was founded and his name possibly lives on at such places as Cheddleton (Chad's Town) as well. The young prince stayed the night at this hermit's cell and the following day brought his brother along. They both became Christians as a result of the preaching and teaching of Chad and were both baptised. Their father was angry and they both had to flee his wrath, moving away from the royal household at Bury Bank, but Wulfere chased them. He caught up with his son Wulfad who had taken refuge at the hermit's cell and killed him and he caught up with Rufin at Burston (its name probably denoting Burial Stone) between Sandon and Stone.

Little can be seen of where the Mercian Kings held their courts at Bury Bank.
This is the desolate scene today.

21

Their mother, the story says, took up their bodies and had them buried underneath "a great heap of stones" or a sepulchre of stones, around the year 670 AD, and this, it is said, is why the township is now called Stone. Queen Ermendilda later had a church dedicated to St Mary and St Wulfad built at the site and utilised these stones within it. This church and a hermitage remained until about 874 and was then partially destroyed, possibly by the Danes who were invading at that time.

Trees as old as time grow at Bury Bank.

As romantic as that story is, I don't think it is the real reason for the town's name. I think the story was invented to disguise the fact that the church and the hermitage were on the site of a sacred stone used by the pagans or the heathens as they were often called. Wulfere, the so-called pagan king, was a Christian at the time of Chad coming to Mercia and the Saint was sent south to Mercia from Northumberland at the request of the King of Mercia – Wulfere – who asked for missionaries to help him convert the people of the upper Trent. It was Ermendilda and Wulfere together who had the church built at Stone and dedicated to St Mary and to one of their sons, who, it should be noticed, had been made a Saint after his death.

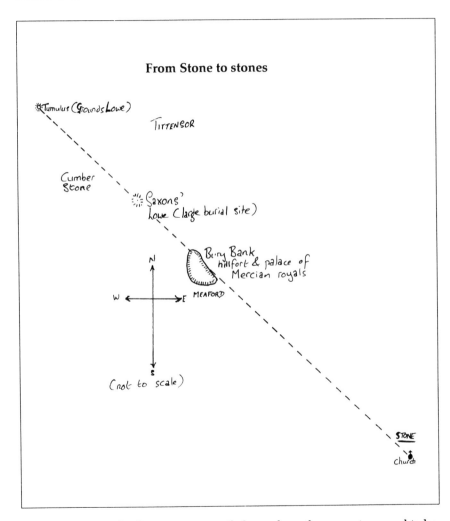

From Stone to stones

A map showing a ley line or energy path from where the monastery used to be at Stone, now the church, through Bury Bank, Saxons Lowe and concluding at Grounds Lowe, a tumulus.

The site on which the original Christian church was built was the site previously used for worshipping the gods of old. And it was marked by a stone, most probably a large monolith of sufficient structure for the town that grew up around it to be named after it. This town was named after a particular stone, not "Stones" as the legend implies.

Pillars of Stone

Whether the King of Mercia, Wulfere, was a pagan or a Christian, is not now the question we need to devote our time to. What we do know for certain is that his daughter, Werburgh or Werburga, most certainly was a Christian for all of her life. She founded many religious houses and centres throughout her father's kingdom of Mercia. When she died her remains were placed in a grave at Repton, and when the Danes attacked Repton in the centre of Mercia in 873 the grave was dug, her relics placed in a small casket and taken to Chester, one of the furthest outposts of the Mercian kingdom. First of all this casket went to Hanbury then was taken to Chester (where the Cathedral is now dedicated to her memory) but during the journey the procession stopped at Trentham. The cross in the churchyard at Trentham is understood to have been built as a praying or penitential station on the exact spot where this Saintly person's remains were rested although there is a possibility that the original cross was destroyed at one time and replaced by the present one. The steps around it are very worn and it is possible these are the original steps, worn away by the feet and the knees of people praying to the Saintly Princess.

There are many stone crosses or pillars at churches throughout Staffordshire and some have had legends or traditions woven around them. And there is one at Wolverhampton that depicts the pagan aspects of our land. In the year 1798 a Staffordshire historian named Shaw wrote: "In the churchyard, almost fronting the south porch, is a round pillar, about twenty feet high, covered with rude carvings, divided into several compartments. On the northwest face, at bottom, in the spandrels of a kind of arch, are cut a bird and a beast, looking back at each other. Above, divided by a narrow band, are other similar figures, or dragons, with fore-feet and long tails, in lozenges. Above them, a band of Saxon leaves, and in lozenges, birds and roses. Over these, a narrow band, and then, in lozenges, beasts and griffins. Another band, and a compartment of rude carvings, and then a regular plain capital. Whether it once supported a cross is uncertain. The bottom of the pillar has stone masonry worked round it to keep it upright. Whether this is a Danish or a Saxon monument is not exactly determined."

A stone monolith, West Park, Wolverhampton (from a picture taken in the 1920s).

The cross at Trentham church. Steps to it have been well-worn by worshippers over the centuries.

The Leek cross that holds a dire warning should it move.

Scholars are undecided as to its origins. It could be Danish, it could be Saxon or it could be Norman, it has been said. Quite a difference. What is more than interesting is the number of dragons depicted. These dragons depicted the earth energy lines, the dragon lines. They were suppressed by the Church in the form of St George defeating the dragon and also St Michael doing likewise. The dragon, or the griffin, is often carved on the sites of converging energy lines. And churches have often been built on these spots over pre-Christian sites.

It has also been said that this cross compares with one in the churchyard of the Parish Church at Leek, at the opposite end of the County. This cross, near the chancel door, is about ten feet in height (roughly three metres) and the steps are well worn, like the steps at Trentham. The interwoven pattern, in a serpentine fashion is prominent and this was probably at that site before the present church was built. In the Gentleman's Magazine of 1780 there was the first record of a tradition associated with this shaft of stone. The tradition has it that the shaft sinks lower into the ground every year and a rhyme says:

"When the Churchyard cross shall disappear
Leek town will not last another year."

Similar crosses are also to be found at Ilam Church and Draycott, Checkley and Chebsey and on private ground at Swythamley Hall. But that is not all. As this book is based on Staffordshire, I won't dwell on the similarity of the three pillars in West Park, Macclesfield, the enigmatic Cleulow Cross stone near to Wincle and the stone in the hedgerow at Upton – all Cheshire; but similar they are in every aspect ... and only a few miles away at that. Tradition says that the cross at Checkley denoted a battle between the Danes and the English at which three Bishops were slain and three great stones were placed in the memorial in their honour. Pattingham, Cheadle and Rocester churchyards also boast crosses and there is an old stone cross at Rushall Church. Perhaps you may know of others.

At the junction of the London road and the Birmingham to Walsall road two miles out of Stafford is Weeping Cross, now denoting a boundary. It is supposed to get its name from the fact that people paid penance for flouting church laws but, more sinister than that, it was the place where Wrongdoers were executed according to the "Natural History of Staffordshire". These sites were, more often than not, at crossroads, and this is no exception. The weepers were, no doubt, the friends and relatives of the hanged person.

We have discussed the Christianisation of primitive sites before, and now we come to yet another example, for at Tixall there is a cross on top of an ancient burial mound – placed there at some point in our history no doubt by a person or persons who wished to sanctify the spot. It is also recorded that it is the site of an assassination and the cross denotes that.

One of the Saxon crosses at Ilam.

There is an area known as Stone Cross in the vicinity of West Bromwich, Walsall and Wednesbury. Tradition has it that there stood a cross on the roadside and there was a shrine at the spot, denoting what we do not know. In 1794 a Minister wrote that he had seen a stone pillar at Stone Cross, and said it was higher and vaster than the kind that sun dials were placed on. There were also two others at one time and there were stone steps.

Mucklestone Mystery

Audley, Madeley, Keele and Castle,
Hixon, Muxon, Woore and Aston,
Ranscliffe is rugged, and Wrinehill is rough,
But Betley's the place where the Devil broke through.

This is a rhyme which comes from Betley, where Staffordhire kisses its County cousins, Cheshire and Shropshire, and it alludes to the terrible state the local roads used to be in (and some would say still are!). The name Muxon is the shortened and localised form of Mucklestone.

Even today, with so much wanton destruction in the name of civilisation, it is still possible to discover a village, hamlet or just a group of dwellings, that has retained the earth spirit within. Such a place is Mucklestone.

This is a village that has saved much that has been lost by many. It is one of the few areas still retaining its Sense of Place. It, and some of its people, know what the earth can still give. It is a spot I have often been drawn to because of the magic blanketing the area. And just by the village there are two stones, ancient when Jesus walked this land, that still retain energy, power and magnetism. They are known as the Devil's Ring and Finger (I have mentioned them briefly before) and they drew me to them through synchronicity, co-incidence or intended coincidence, call it what you will.

Let me explain. The story begins in the most northerly part of Staffordshire, quite a few miles away from Mucklestone but connected quite strongly. I have family ties with Swythamley Hall (not blood ties, but my family were tenants of the Brocklehurst family who lived there) and have often been drawn to that spot, for reasons I am unable to explain, perhaps because of something still in the memory banks of my genes, who knows. I have had the pleasure of meeting the last of the line of the Brocklehurst dynasty, Sir Philip, on several occasions; my father was a drinking buddy of his brother Courtney (shot while on a spying mission in Burma) and after the hall was sold to followers of the Maharishi in the 1970s I was invited there on several occasions; the last time being to witness the Flying Olympics (a genuine attempt to induce a physical state of flying through a mental state of well being). I was impressed by the genuine belief the followers of that Holy Man had; a belief in both him and in themselves, but Concorde has little to fear from their attempts to fly ... at least for the time being.

Then, lo and behold, the next owner of the Hall, Mr Richard Naylor, extended an invitation for me to visit him at the Hall. There, I was able to see the Knights Low – an ancient burial mound – within the grounds, look at the mysterious stone heads in the walls of the Hall and see the ancient royal seals in the possession of Mr Naylor. This is where there once stood the hunting lodge of the Earls of Chester (and where one of the noble earls wished his heart to be buried) and where, undoubtedly in my view, the saga of Gawain and the Green Knight was set. But I'm digressing. In February of 1994 I was shown a number of photographs that Sir Philip had handed on shortly before his sad passing (and some of them are reproduced in this book). One showed the memorial stone cross at Blore Heath, depicting the spot where the Lancastrian army came to grief in 1459 during the Wars of the Roses, and the other showed the Devil's Ring and Finger on land belonging to Arbour Farm, Mucklestone. How Sir Philip came by them I know not; he may even have taken the photographs himself. I do know that his father's name was Lancaster Brocklehurst and so, presumably, his ancestors fell at Blore Heath and this would account for the photo of the memorial stone ... but why the Devil's Ring? Whatever the reason, I am very pleased that he did pass the photo on for not only did it spur me on, after looking at them, to travel to magical Mucklestone but it also enabled me to display within this book a photograph of the Devil's Ring and Finger. Today the Ring and Finger stand on private land, heavily fenced off, and it is well nigh impossible to get a decent photograph from the footpath a good thirty or so feet away. And my visit there led me to the discovery of a stone circle where I found a clear attempt to Christianise this circle with the carving of the Calvary Cross.

At Knights Low. The cross on the top has been placed there in more recent times. The pillar itself is identical to at least six others in the area.

The Devil's Ring and Finger at Mucklestone from an old photograph by Sir Philip Brocklehurst. These two stones are now against a drystone wall (courtesy Joyce Matthews).

More about the Devil's Ring and Finger

The Devil's Ring and Finger dating back some 2000 years (map reference SJ 707379) comprises of two large stones. The one known as the Ring is, quite obviously, circular, with a hole through the middle; rather like the millstones that mark the boundaries of the Peak Park, and is 1.8 metres from side to side and 1.2 metres tall. The Finger is the same height as the Ring is wide and its own width is about 0.9 metres. They now virtually form a part of the wall dividing Arbour Farm and the Oakley Estate. The boundary is heavily fenced and it is not possible to get near these stones today; barbed wire forbids it. However, a footpath or bridleway goes pretty close and it is possible to view them. According to James Dyer's book "Prehistoric England and Wales" published by Penguin, 1981, it is probable they were part of a burial chamber and are unlikely to be in their original positions. How correct this is.

And I wonder if, in fact, they should be positioned together. The circular stone was used for one of two purposes, either as a sighting stone whereby the sun, moor or stars could be seen through the hole or as a healing stone whereby a limb or even a head was placed in it and the power emanating from the stone aided the sick person. Or it could have been used for both, being aligned to (most probably) the sunrise at a certain solstice and then used for healing when the sun rose on that day and the afflicted people could gain the benefit of the extra pulse of the earth at that time. Local tradition has it that mothers passed their sick children through it to cure them.

And what, therefore, of the "Finger"? This is a stone that was in all probability one of many at a circle of stones and the Devil's Ring was used at that self-same circle, and it could have been used for alignment with the Ring or without it. But where was that circle?

The answer is easy.

As you walk along the pathway that leads from just beyond the lodge houses of Oakley Hall you can, after about a quarter of a mile, see the Devil's Ring and Finger to the right. Just to the left (and still keeping on the path) there can be viewed a mound that has been bedecked with trees. Around this mound there are still a number of stones that form an ovoid and there is obviously a good number of them missing. They have been removed just as the Ring and Finger have, possibly hundreds of years ago. However, there is another clue to where this possible burial chamber or circle may have been sited, for on some of these stones there are markings. Some of the markings are, quite clearly, crosses. Yet another example of the Christianisation of the Earth Religions. And don't let us forget that the hole and the long stone have obvious female and male sexual connotations. Could this have had fertility cult implications?

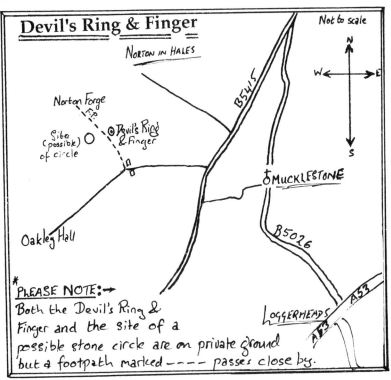

Please keep to the footpath ... the Ring and Finger and the circle of stones can be seen from the path.

As I have already mentioned, Mucklestone is full of magic. And it has been for many centuries. The story has been told of a black-

35

smith from that vicinity who was very much alive in the 1870s and had the nickname of The Bloodstopper. His Christian names was Charles and the local dialect had him as Owd Charles, for he was in his eighties by then, and he had the gift of healing animals, especially those that were badly bleeding, by quoting a passage from the Bible. That was all, and his gift was much sought after. And it worked.

Tradition has it that Queen Margaret witnessed the Battle of Blore Heath from the tower of Mucklestone Church and afterwards, her footprints remained in the stone floor there.

As we walked along the footpath we noticed a circle of stones to our left. This stone was just by the path. It had a cross carved into it. I placed soil in the grooves so it would show up better on a photograph.

Cross on stone, near Devil's Ring and Finger

36

Other Stones and Circles

There are more stones and circles and burial mounds in our fair County and these are spotlighted in various chapters. The area around Ilam Moor and Alstonefield, for instance, has an elegance of cairns but many were excavated by Thomas Bateman and also by Samuel Carrington, and they managed to destroy some of the earth energy in the process, but it still hangs on and can still be experienced. Then there is Kinver Hill Fort above the River Stour; Castle Ring standing majestically over Cannock Chase; Berth Hill at Maer and Berry Ring at Bradley ... all wonders in their own right. Do, please, visit them if you are able. You will be the richer for it.

On the eve of the Dissolution of the Monasteries, I wonder if the Monks of the Cistercian Order at Croxden Abbey hid their most holy of relics – an ancient stone?

In 1905, Stepehensons, quarry owners of nearby Hollington, decided to quarry for "Red Hollington" stone and set about opening out a new working at a spot where, they believed, the stone for Croxden Abbey was obtained. They came upon a "bench" in the old workings and after the removal of much refuse they found lying at full length the shaft of an ancient upright cross some seven feet in length.

This was not a half-completed cross or anything like that, it was magnificently carved and as old as the Abbey, if not older. What stories could that stone tell, I wonder.

Stones of every shape and size, some carved and some in their natural state, have been venerated by Staffordshire people for as long as people have been worshipping. Stories and traditions have grown up around many and, in some cases, stories and traditions have been lost. What, for instance, is the real truth behind the stone at Norton in Hales? The stone has stood for centuries facing the church and was said by a writer for the North Staffs Field Club in 1923 that it appeared to be the capstone of a prehistoric burial place. This stone was of such importance at one time that a church was sited next to it; the stone had been there countless centuries before the Christian Church came and was it, I wonder, a spot where worship took place before the Christians came to our shores. A church grew by it as did a community.

Stones in various carved forms have appeared at churches; some were there before the church, others came afterwards. There were various fragments of ornamental stones found at Alstonefield, undoubtedly pre-Norman. There is a restored cross at Cheddleton Church, a broken cross at Ferny Hill and a cross at Cheddleton Heath. The list goes on.

The stone now known as Shepherds Cross on Biddulph Moor. It has obviously been carved into a cross at some date and stands across from a well and the site of a possible Druids Grove.

At the Devil's Hole

Before we leave the stones of Staffordshire we must pause awhile at the beautiful area of the Coombes Valley now a Sanctuary for birdlife controlled by the R.S.P.B. This is well worth a visit whether or not you are a lover of birdlife. It is a spot where nature has taken nothing but given everything, a spot where the earth spirit is still roaming. The entire area stretching to Ipstones (itself an area of stone magic for its own name is devoted to rock worship or rock usage) is a delight to all the senses, including the sixth sense. Within the Coombes Valley Nature Reserve there is, now hidden and overgrown, a spot known as The Devil's Hole. It is so called because it was connected with earth worship at one time, not Devil Worship as we know today. Anything not Christian was, as I have pointed out before, of the Devil in the eyes of the Church.

Thanks to the kindness of the staff at the R.S.P.B. Reserve I and Hilary were taken to the Horsley Stone. The large stone to the right and the stone in the river were one but have been broken into two at some time.

In the book "Tales of Ipstones" by the Rev. F. Brightman and published in 1937 is the story of Horsley's Stone in this valley. He tells the tale that two brothers named Horsley were cared for by a young housekeeper because their mother had died. Both fell in love with her and one slew the other and threw his body in the Coombe Stream. To hide the body he threw down a rocking stone from above and this is now called Horsley's Stone.

The story goes that Horsley's ghost was laid there in the form of a bird which was in accordance with the request of the unhappy ghost. Many old people claim to have seen the bird and listened at the close of day to its sad and plaintive song. A poacher was fishing and the bird ghost appeared; after entering the door of the lantern which the poacher had opened for greater light the bird put out the light of the candle then flew to the bushes nearby and began its melancholy song.

The poet and self-styled Seeker of the Grail, Ralph de Tunstall Sneyd, who wrote about Horsley's Stone and its haunting is on this picture of a Druid ceremony going to Thor's Cave in the Manifold Valley in 1933. The lady second from left is holding the Horn of Plenty and Ralph is fourth from left with a white band on his hood (picture courtesy of Sandra Burgess).

There is another version of this, told by a quite remarkable character called Ralph de Tunstall Sneyd. I wrote about this self-styled Seeker of the Grail in my book "Magic, Myth and Memories" and refer to him again within these chapters. Ralph was a mystic and a Seeker of the Truth, his own Holy Grail. He wrote the following poem, in which he gives a slightly differing version of the legend, saying that after the murder the body was burned and the ghost roamed the home and twelve churchpeople tried to exorcise the ghost but eleven of them were so scared they fled, leaving just one who laid the ghost to rest under the stone. This is his poem:

In the fair valley of the Coomb
The fox and magpie find a home
The lapwing to his mate does call
When the high sun shines on Sharpcliffe Hall
But the Devil's Hole is a place of fear,
A spirit wild is prisoned here.
A great black stone the place doth mark
And round it whirl the waters dark,
And boiling eddies round it surge
As the wild wind howls a funeral durge.
And chains are heard in the star-lit night
When the owl flits by and the moon shines bright.
For, in a house not far away,
Two brothers lived, so the old men say;
And one was skilled in healing art,
The other bore a lawyer's part.
The doctor deadly poisons mixed
For on his brother's death he fixed.
And then, the fearful deed to hide,
He burnt the corpse in an oven wide,
But the foul sin he could not screen,
For still his brother's ghost was seen.
But twelve divines together pray
And strive the troubled ghost to lay,
And all but one in terror fly,
But he resolves his task to ply.
And still he prays with trembling hands,

Till down his face the sweat descends.
At last the awful task is done,
And the spirit lies beneath the stone.
But still a wondrous bird is seen,
Hovering near in the forest green.

This legend of ghosts and exorcism gives an explanation for the naming of the stone; but surely Horsley means either the "old" stone in the clearing or "boundary" stone in the clearing. Either way the stone is special, for if it is named because of its antiquity it has been venerated by many and if it has been used as a boundary mark it has, likewise, been a special stone. Whatever the reason there are spirits at the place. Earth spirits.

3

Haunted Staffordshire

The worship of ancestors was most probably one of the first forms of religion. Awareness of those who have gone before has, quite obviously, been prevalent in the human memory since we came down from the trees and visualisation conjured from the memory banks has always been easy. The earliest known ancestors of ours buried their dead – at least the most venerated of their dead – with much ceremony and it has always been a mainstay of worship and religion of whatever creed that there is either life after death or the souls of those departed will return again – reincarnated, in some other body. Ancestor worship meant those who had passed on became gods, albeit of a minor nature, and this gave them powers above and beyond mere mortals. They came to be guardians of the community, beings or entities to be called upon in time of need. To primitive people it was necessary to keep these entities happy and so they were showered with praises (now called prayers) and were given gifts, often at great personal sacrifice ... becoming the sacrificial gifts. After all, if they became angry and didn't help any more then goodness knew what would happen; animals could become sick, crops could fail and enemies of the community could attack and be successful.

As societies became more complex then the happy hunting grounds of the ancestors, in the form of Valhalla or whatever other afterworld it may have been, became more and more distinct and divorced from the here and now. These Elysian Fields were where the souls of the departed craved for and where they should go, only sometimes it wasn't always plain sailing on the ferry across the River Styx ... a murder or suicide left the soul in torment, and sometimes the murder victim had to harass those still on the earth plain until the time that revenge was sweet.

It was also important to bury the bodies of the dead in the proper manner or else their spirits could not find their way to the heavenly resting places; and it was equally important to make sure the journey was a happy and contented one, with offerings being made at the graveside and, in earlier times, servants and favourite pets being buried alongside them. Just look at how the Pharaohs of Egypt were interred, and Neolithic people went to their graves with weapons, ornaments for bartering and in many cases a jug of beer or other alcoholic brew to assist.

People who see ghosts

These primitive attitudes towards the spirits or souls of the departed were kept alive over the centuries and our folklore and popular culture has ensured that these ghosts of the past remain to haunt us.

And, of course, there have always been those who can genuinely 'see' the dead. Just pay a visit to one of our present-day Spiritualist Churches or have a word with a Medium. I have experienced this myself on many occasions and even met my father shortly after he died ... let me tell you about it.

I and Hilary had gone to bed at our home in Rudyard in North Staffordshire and I was awoken at about 3 a.m. by the feeling that there was someone in the room. I immediately thought we were being burgled, especially when my bleary eyes began to focus on a figure standing at the foot of the bed. I shouted some expletive or other and switched on the light and saw my father. "What the hell are you doing here?" I shouted and his figure slowly disappeared. Just then the front door bell rang. I scrambled out of bed and went to answer it. A policeman stood at the door. "I'm sorry to tell you that your father has died," he told me. Then what about the followers of the Roman Catholic faith who have seen the Virgin Mary or a Saint? And don't the Aborigines of Australia still hold conversations with their ancestors and sit down to meals with them? The North American Indians, Spiritualists before that religion was formed, speak to their departed. And so it goes ...

One of the most famous of Staffordshire's sons, Samuel 'Dictionary' Johnson, once said that the subject of ghosts was "one of the most important that can come before the human understanding." Is is, he said, a question which, after five thousand years, is yet undecided. Almost everyone has their own tale to tell of a ghost or haunting experience; if it did not happen to them personally then they know of someone who did experience it.

The "haunted" bedroom at Swythamley Hall. The ghost of a mistress of a member of the de Trafford family walked here, it is said, searching for the baby she lost during childbirth. (courtesy Joyce Matthews).

A Walsall ghost?

At the White Hart Inn at Caldmore Green in Walsall, the mummified arm and hand of a child was found along with a seventeenth century sword in the loft. It later found its way to the Central Library at Walsall. There have been a number of theories about how it came to be at the inn, and a number of people are convinced it has connections with witchcraft, or, more to the point, with the worship of the black arts. It was proved to be the kind used by teaching hospitals and contained chemical preservative. It is believed a young girl committed suicide some 170 or more years ago and, like so many suicides, it is said that her soul cannot find peace (suicides were buried in unconsecrated ground or at crossroads) and it still haunts the area. Whether this arm was taken from the body of a girl who committed suicide is not clear. Back in the year 1955 the print of a small hand was discovered in the dust on a table that was kept in the attic of the inn. Some years later the then licensee saw a ghostly apparition at his bedside.

Many buildings throughout Staffordshire have tales of hauntings. This old picture shows the Co-op on Buxton Road, Leek, where strange sounds were often heard and, at one time, an errand boy fled after he saw a ghost of an old man with a long grey beard.

Some members of a local Paranormal Society decided to spend a night there and saw nothing although they did report that the

46

atmosphere showed something paranormal did exist there and, as is so often the case, it was a lot colder there than elsewhere. Another manager of the pub reported someone pacing up and down in the attic, which he found to be empty. His dog growled and its hairs bristled.

Most towns and villages have tales of ghosts and hauntings. In North Staffordshire, for instance, there is the Jewel in the Crown of the Moorlands, Leek, and a village close by called Ipstones that boasts many a haunting tale. Let me tell you a few.

Poltergeist co-incidence

I had the pleasure of giving a talk to a number of people of Leek back in January of 1994 and afterwards a lady came up to me and asked me if I knew about the haunted house in Ball Haye Road. I told her I didn't and she related to me how this terraced cottage was haunted or troubled by a poltergeist. Apparently three sisters, all spinsters, had lived there and one of them brought home a gentleman friend. Immediately things started to fly about, saucepans fell to the floor, pictures went askew, lights switched on and off ... obviously the presence of a male in the household was not welcomed by something.

And that was that. I registered it in the back of my mind for further reference at a future date and left it at that. The very next person I spoke to, a charming lady in her forties, asked me: "Have you heard about the poltergeist in Ball Haye Road? Coincidence, yes; synchronicity, yes. Those two had never met, they had come across the phenomenon years apart ... I left them comparing notes.

The Cavalier

Then there was the gentleman who told me about the Cavalier of Dicky's Gutter. Now Dicky's Gutter is a small road or passageway, locals would call it an Entry, close by the offices of the Staffordshire Moorlands District Council. It leads to the park from the main Manchester to Derby trunk route. He told me of when he had seen, walking along the passageway, the apparition of a man dressed like a Cavalier complete with flowing black wig, fancy clothes and a rapier sword.

Ghosts leave no footprints?

My father, who appeared to me as a ghost on the morning of his death, himself saw a ghost when he was driving a travelling shop van for the Rudyard firm of Abberleys in the 1950s. These travelling shops visited the lonely farms and houses of the Staffordshire moorlands and were always made welcome by the locals. Communications were not as good in those days as today and some of these isolated homes had very few visitors. There was always a cup of tea and a chat on offer and many was the time when the travelling shop served as a local bus service as well, taking an occupant of one farm to another farm or a house along the route. So one afternoon, in a blinding snowstorm, it would not have been unusual for him to have offered a lift to an elderly lady walking past the Royal Cottage in Quarnford. Especially in the conditions that prevailed with the snowfall getting worse and darkness about to set in. "Do you want a lift?" he asked the old lady trudging along in the snow. "Yes please" she replied and walked around the back of the van to get into the passenger seat of the cab. My father waited and waited and then feared that she had perhaps fallen in the snow so he got out. There was no-one to be seen but her footprints came to an abrupt stop by the cab door. Pretty soon the falling snow and driving wind covered the tracks. He searched around as best he could but he never saw the lady again.

Charms and spells

Throughout the length and breadth of Staffordshire people have been frightened by the thoughts of the unknown, of spectres, ghosts, spirits, call them what you will, and they have had their own charms and incantations to ward them off. Some still carry charms and have incantations to ward them off – perhaps in the form of a crucifix and a prayer. A Vicar of Ipstones, for instance, was certainly not feared of these visitations and he most certainly had no qualms about writing of them. The Rev. F. Brighton wrote a fascinating book "A Tale of Ipstones" in 1937 and in it he told a number of ghostly tales. He wrote, for instance, of a Spinney not far from the Red Lion at Ipstones Edge on the road to Bottom House. At that spot people have felt the presence of, and seen, the ghost of a young woman murdered and buried there. The body was discovered because of the dreams, or should they be called nightmares, of her mother. Near the same place four different people have said to have seen what appeared to be three different people standing over a bicycle which, as they approached, all vanished.

He also told of strange happenings back in 1916 during the first world war at a 300 years old farmhouse known as The Hermitage. It got its name, he said, because of an old miser who lived there and who hoarded his wealth. It was believed that this stooped old man with a tall hat haunted the building. People have experienced the feeling of a wind passing by accompanied by a rustling noise.

A servant heard ghostly screams under the window and a cousin of the household lay in bed and heard the sound of an organ playing downstairs. There were favourite times for the hauntings to take place: Easter, Whit, Good Friday, Christmas and at hay-making time and at one of these times an unoccupied bed was heard to move. Also, a large dog has been seen on many occasions at the end of the lane leading to the building. One man kicked out at the beast but his foot touched nothing. A light was seen to wander down the lane one night, going towards the farm. And then it vanished. On another evening the family were in the kitchen when they heard a sound like a hundred planks of wood falling over. The planks were there but intact.

The Churchyard ghost

And then there is the Ipstones churchyard ghost. There had been a social evening at the village school and a young man was on his way home to Clerk's Bank just after midnight. He was just passing a few yards past the churchyard corner when he found his way barred by something invisible. He neither saw nor heard anything and he lifted his foot to step forward but could not. He turned back as far as the two cottages by the church gate and then turned back and made another attempt. At the same spot he was stopped again, there was no pressure or touch, he simply could not obey his will to go forward. He turned back again and went home over the fields.

There is a stone nearby to Ipstones, by the name of Horsley's Stone, and it is said to be haunted by a tiny bird. I have told more of this in another chapter for there are connections with earth energies and the power of stones within this tale and here we wish to hear of ghosts ...

Black Country warning

Wherever someone has met their death in horrible or suspicious circumstances their ghosts have remained in the minds of people. At Tunstall, for instance, there walks the ghost of a teenager hanged for murder and the miners of Staffordshire have always had their tales of the spectres of the coalfields. Miss Amy Lyons wrote a good number of years ago in "Black Country Sketches" of an eighteenth century scene in the Cockfighters Arms at Wednesbury. A party of colliers had adjourned to the pub after being driven from the pit by fearful sounds they had heard down in the black depths of the mine. An old miner by the name of Ribber is reported as saying to his employer named Butty in a glorious Black Country accent: "Thee cosn't say thee hasn't been warned Ode Gabriel has been aboute with hissen hounds pretty nigh all this wick an todee thee couldsta eerd 'em fine a yelpin'."

Miss Lyons wrote that over the chimney breast on a large painted boards was "Ye Colliers Guide of Signs and Warnings" and listed:

To dream of a broken shoe, a sure sign of danger.
If you mete a woman at the rising of ye sun, turne again from ye pit, a sure sign of death.
To dreame of a fire is a sure sign of danger.
To see a bright light in ye mine is a warning to flee away.
If Gabriel's Hounds ben aboute, doe not worke that day.
When foule smells be aboute ye pit, a sure sign that ye imps an bin annear.
To charm away ghosts and ye lik: Take a Bible and a key, hold both in ye right hand and say ye Lord's prayer and they will right speedily get farre away.

50

A collier would not, in addition to these warnings, descend the pit if he encountered a cross-eyed woman on his way to the pit or if he saw a robin on a wall or other artificial object.

Whistling in the dark

And then there were The Whistlers, a warning of disaster if the sound of whistling was heard about the pit mouth. In the North of Staffordshire the same omen was known as the Seven Whisperers. Dr Plot wrote in "The History of Staffordshire": "We need go no further than Wednesbury for an instance of unknown noises. The colliers there will tell you that early in the morning as they go to the collepitt they sometimes hear the noise of a pack of hounds in the air, which happens so frequently that they have a name for them, calling them Gabriel's Hounds, though the more sober folks take them to be wild geese making a noise in their flight."

Often, the tales of ghosts have been handed down through sheer fear of the unknown. On a bleak moorland where the traveller had to cross on his own there was many a tale of a spirit luring the unwary traveller to his fate. Could this, I wonder, have been a deliberate attempt to tell those travellers that danger lurked in the fogbound bogs?

The peat bog

Nearby to Stowe there is a 104 acre bog called Chartley Moss, a place of danger to this day. It comprises of a raft of peat some three metres thick that is floating on a lake of water to a depth of fifteen metres or more. This is a place where legends abound and is an area full of mystery fed by the imagination. A ghostly apparition of a huntsman followed by a pack of hounds rides this spot. Countless people have, over the centuries, come to grief in this area and many items from swords to carts and horses to dogs have vanished. It is now in the hands of the Nature Conservancy and if you are brave enough to want to experience this spot then you must go on a guided tour led by someone from this team. Do not, under any circumstances, attempt to go there on your own.

This is a tradition at Yoxall that a blacksmith's apprentice committed suicide because he was so badly treated by his master. As with all suicides at one time, he was buried in an unconsecrated grave and the story is that no horse will ever pass by that spot. There is also the story that at a tumulus (an ancient burial ground) there was unearthed the skeleton of a boy who had been speared to death and this, it is said, is the same spot where no horse will go past. I fear that both traditions have merged into one at some point.

Bingo!

And, more up to date, we are told of the Bingo Hall ghost at Longton in the Potteries. In the early 1970s, when so many former cinemas had been converted to large halls at which bingo was played, there lurked the tale of a member of staff falling over the balcony and breaking his neck in the fall. The caretaker during the year 1971 was Mr Alfred Newman and one night he saw a figure glide across the balcony. He bravely went towards it and saw it to be a man of middle age who was dressed in darkly coloured clothing and he described the figure as gliding in and out of the front row of seats. But it didn't end there for a couple of days later Mr Newman saw this self same spectre again at the same place. He had his dog with him this time and the caretaker shouted at the apparition which disappeared at that moment. Mr Newman said the figure was bending over the rails when it disappeared and his guard dog was very distressed, its fur was bristling.

On the B5026 road between Loggerheads and Eccleshall, south of Newcastle under Lyme, there is the tiny yet mystical village of Broughton. Opposite the lovely church of St Peters is Broughton Hall, a wonderful place that has been described as being the most spectacular piece of black and white architecture in this country. It comes as little or no surprise that a mansion of this stature should boast a ghost, but the name given to it doesn't quite fit the elegance of the hall. The name of this spirit is Red Socks. The exterior of this fine hall has a history going back to the year 1637 and some time between then and now, so the story goes, a servant woman from Broughton was in the Long Gallery attic cleaning the staircase and she sensed that someone was standing over her. She glanced up and saw a "young man" walking down the stairs towards her. She got up off her knees to let him pass and thought she had better move her bucket full of mucky water out of the way as well. But there was no need, he walked straight through her. This young man was wearing bright red socks, she noticed, and so the nickname was given. There is more to tell of this hamlet ... a place haunting in more ways than ghostly ... for just off the road that passes through the village is Charnes Hall, the home of the Vernon Yonge family until 1916. For centuries there has been told the tale of the phantom of a woman said to be searching for her wedding ring stolen from her finger by a servant woman as she lay in her coffin. Many people who have seen her describe her as wearing flowing silken gowns and, it is said, she is affectionately known as Silky because of this.

Some seven miles south of Stafford at Little Haywood there is a bridge known locally as Weetman's Bridge, and at one time Wheatman's Bridge. Whether it is named after one person or named after the fact that wheat was carried over it is uncertain but it is said to be a haunted spot. There has been seen, and indeed heard, the ghost of a woman weeping. Did she drown after jumping off that spot I wonder?

There is a private farmhouse at Bloxwich called Hills House Farm and it has been widely reported that at certain times of the year a sharp cracking noise is heard in the bedroom and footsteps are heard in the same bedroom. It is also said that on one Sunday every month a figure is seen gliding through the living room.

Four miles to the west of Stafford is the village of Haughton and here is the ghost of a maid of a very tidy disposition: at The Moat House there is a room that is always kept dust-free by this spectre; a very handy ghost to have if you must have one at all ...

Return of the Soldier

There are countless tales of ghosts and spectres haunting Stafford-shire; every town and every village has at least one to tell. Some are more famous than others and some are not well known at all because people wish to keep the fact that their home is haunted well and truly to themselves. It is not the sort of thing most people wish to broadcast to the nation but, there again, others are only too pleased to do so. Legends and traditions thrive on a tale or two told on a dark and foggy night around a crackling log fire; that environment is a happy haunting ground for the spirits to come into the open minds of people.

Let me tell the tale of Slade Man's Hole. This spot is about one and a half miles from Draycott and local tradition has it that there was once a battle at this place and a number of soldiers were killed and buried here. Perhaps the spelling of its name should be Slayed Man's Hole. The local tradition states that if anything is thrown at the rocks then a soldier appears. It can be likened to many traditions up and down the county and indeed across the country where the same thing is said to happen. Please chuck a stone at the rocks and see if you can spot a spirit soldier ... I have been told the tale of a young girl who had been sent to Tean to get some medicine for a relative and on her return she, like all the children in the neighbourhood, automatically threw a stone at the rocks of Slade Man's Hole. She immediately heard a noise and so she ran as though the Hounds of Hell were after her. When she arrived home, breathless and in great shock, she realised that the noise she heard was the pop of a cork on the bottle of medicine she was carrying.

The list is endless ... there is the spectre of an old man seen at a steel scaffolding factory at Leek whose presence is always heralded by the smell of pipe tobacco; the ghost of a young girl who walks by the Cathedral at Lichfield and the vision of a young man is often seen at Wychnor walking the fields ... in search of his lost love, it is said.

And there are the ghosts of the slain at Blore Heath, where the Lancastrian army was defeated and many hundreds slain during the Civil War; many lost souls still walk that spot, where a stone cross has been erected, tradition says.

Blore Heath cross from one of Sir Philip Brocklehurst's old pictures
(Joyce Matthews).

4

Staffordshire Waters of Life

Pilgrimage to Ladydale

On a crisp Saturday morning in February of 1964, six people went on a pilgrimage.

They took the path trodden by the feet of thousands over centuries of time; their goal was a healing well where the waters had ceased to flow thanks to the evils of Adolph Hitler.

Let me explain.

In the North Staffordshire township of Leek there is an area known as Ladydale, now an area of delightful modern houses but there are still a few fields in the vicinity, thank goodness. Ladydale nestles in a valley by the side of a fairly new church dedicated to All Saints. Through this valley there flows a stream and by this waterway there stands a structure known locally as the Holy Well or Healing Well and, sometimes, Our Lady's Well. It is now a Victorian edifice erected in the 1850s in memory of the son of the then owners of nearby Pickwood Hall. It was built on the site of what had been a holy well or a well worshipped for its healing properties for countless centuries. Just what the well looked like before the Victorian re-building we do not know but it is highly probable that the stones used as the base for the present day structure were the originals, used, as the name implies, as a "well". It later had others added to its top. When it was converted to a shrine in honour of the heir to Pickwood Hall it became more a fountain than a well because the healing waters flowed through the mouth of a metal lion's head placed on the side. All around the structure there were metal railings. However, during the Second

World War the lion's head was probably removed and so were many of the railings – although some around the ceremonial walkway to the healing waters are still intact albeit very rusty and uncared for.

The author (right) assisting during the "pilgrimage" to Ladydale Well.

The very name of Ladydale implies it has been a holy place dedicated to Our Lady the Virgin Mary when Christianity came to these shores but in all probability dedicated to the Earth Mother long before then. It would have been, to these early people, Mother Earth who gave out her healing juices for the benefit of her children, probably the Celtic and pre-Celtic peoples of this magical area. Another aspect of this place is the location of trees nearby, in this instance the ancient woodlands known as Ballington Woods, for according to Janet and Colin Bord in their extremely informative work "Sacred Waters" (Paladin Books 1986) this is a relic of ancient tree worship which once may have been as important as water worship. And just above this ancient woodland there is an area known as Lowe Hill, an ancient burial place. A person sensitive to the psychic who journeyed through the wood told me he found the area around Lowe Hill spiritually uplifting.

Ladydale Well

This is the area where, in all probability, the Cistercian monks were told to come to found an Abbey before they built Dieulacres a mile or so north on the banks of the River Churnet. According to the Chronicles of Dieulacres Abbey related by the Reverend Michael Fisher (a Leek lad) in his scholarly publications "Dieulacres Abbey" first published in 1969 and still going strong, the monks came to this area from Poulton near Chester because of the ever present threats of invasion by the Welsh. He relates that the

58

Chronicles also state that the Earl of Chester, Ranulph de Blundeville, had a dream during which he saw his grandfather's ghost, Ranulph II, who told him to go to "Cholpesdale in the vicinity of Leek" and there establish a community of Cistercian monks "at a place where there had once been a chapel dedicated to the Blessed Virgin Mary."

Was this place Ladydale? Was there once a chapel dedicated to the Blessed Virgin Mary at Ladydale? I certainly think so. The Abbey was eventually built at a site a couple of miles north, as we know. But it was not unusual for minds to be changed for the monks who built Croxden Abbey, also in North Staffordshire, had first of all set about building it at what has now become the village of Alton. And the Earl of Chester had decided to build a castle at Alderley Edge and then changed his mind, or had his mind changed for him, and work stopped at the area still known as Castle Rocks and was transferred to Beeston where the remains of a fine defensive structure still stand proud. Maybe in all these instances the masons – that elite band who handed down their secrets from father to son, decided that the site chosen was not correct for one very particular reason – the earth energy lines were not right for the purpose intended.

Healing waters

The Abbey of Dieulacres is set beside a cave where there was undoubtedly a chapel as well. This site was "dowsed" by myself, my son Charles and a good friend named Mike Oldham (who also accompanied us on our "dig" at Ladydale) and referred to in one of my previous books; but this chapel was always known as the Hermit's Chapel, or the Hermit's Cave, and local tradition stands for a lot, I am convinced. The Chapel dedicated to Our Lady is still kept alive in the name of the area – Ladydale. As for "Cholpesdale", the passing of time has lost its meaning but it was certainly a "Dale" or valley. So is Ladydale.

Within living memory the nearby Catholic Church used the healing waters for the benefit of its flock. There are, at the time of writing this book, a few people in Leek who can remember proces-

and used for healing the sick. Local weavers bathed their eyes there, also.

In the New Year of 1994 I was asked by a group of people living in the Leek area to give a talk to like-minded folk, based on one of my previous works "Magic, Myths and Memories". I was delighted to do so, but unsure of how many would turn up on a wet and windy January evening. I am delighted to report that such a large number came that several had to sit on the floor as all the seats were taken, and many had to stand. Unfortunately many had to be turned away as well because the large function room at The Swan Hotel would not accommodate them. This was not the fault of the Swan proprietors for the function room is more than adequate and is most probably the largest such room in the township but there was, quite simply, a demand that exceeded supply. Such is the interest in Leek and the Moorlands about the hidden aspects of the area. During that evening I met some delightful people and as a result I was asked to accompany a handful of them to the site of Our Lady's Well at Ladydale where I was to dowse for earth energy lines.

But there was a lot more to it than that.

The reason these kind people wished the area to be dowsed was because of the lifelong wish of a charming and devout spinster lady who lives nearby. This wonderful person, in her nineties, had grown up in the area and had been a lifelong worshipper at the nearby church. She was the daughter of a Preacher and she dearly wished to partake of Leek's healing and holy waters but the well had "run dry" many years previously. This dear lady wished her large and rambling house to be left as a Healing Sanctuary when she passed on and this charitable act would enhance the Ladydale healing powers considerably.

And so I and Hilary and a few of these kindly Leekensians went to the site one Sunday morning in that winter. Permission had been obtained from the landowner for us to visit the site (I must emphasise the land is most certainly very private) and the dowsing rods immediately showed the reason for the well being placed where it is. There was not one but FOUR earth energy lines converging on the site and any water flowing through it would undoubtedly have been charged with considerable power because of this. However, there was no water flowing through because the man-made watercourse to it had been diverted into the nearby stream and the hole through which the healing waters once travelled was blocked.

We visited the dear lady after our investigations and told her of our findings. She emphasised how she longed for the holy water to flow again and asked us all to pray (at her shrine in the main bedroom) for this to come about. As we all stood before the altar she had erected, bedecked with pictures of her family and relics from various holy places, she asked me to lead the prayers. I and most of the others present were aware of the enormous spiritual energy that existed around that shrine, energy placed there by this lady who had prayed before it day in and day out for many decades. There were many "ghosts" or "spirits" with us as well (including her own mother) as we prayed and as we stood in silence before the altar.

We all vowed to do something more if we were able. The first task was to gain permission from the owners to attempt to get the waters flowing again and this permission was readily forthcoming. One of the group, Linda Skellam, a reflexologist, a healer in her own right, visited the solicitors acting for the owner and he was able to confirm our mission was acceptable.

So back we went.

The weather was on our side on the twelfth of February, 1994. The sun shone and much of the mud that had hampered us when we first visited had dried to some extent although our wellies still got stuck in the bog many times.

It was immediately obvious that the first thing to do was to unblock the one inch hole through which the waters would eventually flow (we hoped). However, there was an iron bar firmly stuck inside and we assumed this was to block the flow. We then set about clearing the stones of grass and weeds and brambles that had been growing over them, no doubt since the second world war. But what to do next? Inspiration was most certainly needed because we could not remove the metal, despite the spirited attempts of Neil, one of the group who was utilising his car maintenance tools for the project. We had dammed up the water that flowed at the back of the well hoping that the "pond" would act as a reservoir to gravity-feed the outlet but to no avail. A minute or two's reflection was most certainly needed and a much needed rest on our shovels and sticks was eagerly taken.

We all went back to work with a vengeance, none knowing what the others had decided upon, but we had all decided upon the same course of action.

The rear of the structure needed clearing and our spades set to work, cutting through the sods of earth and the tree roots and eventually another piece of metal was unearthed. It became obvious that the metal bar in the hole was connected to this and it became equally obvious that it was a crude form of tap. Push the metal in the hole and the flat metal at the rear moved back and allowed the water to flow through. It had been bent and twisted to block off the hole but it was clear how it had been intended to be used originally and we were able to clear the passage through once we worked this out. We cleared a way for the water to be diverted into the back of the well and then, to our joy, we saw a trickle through the outlet. For the first time since the war against Hitler water was flowing again, albeit a trickle. A garden cane was placed through the outlet and this cleared the backlog of silt, grass and weeds and we cheered as the healing waters gushed out. The water was entering at the back of the well and flowing through the convergence of four earth energy lines and emerging as a powerful source of healing once again. We had done it. Over four hours had been spent – a mere blip in time – and the healing well had returned to do what it had done for countless years. We all bathed our hands in the flowing substance and then we all stood and we all stared and we all said nothing. We subsequently learned that the water used to flow from below there and the hole we unblocked was a 'lever' but, nevertheless, it had worked!

The valley we were in became filled with a vivacity that had not been there a few hours previously. There was an energy all about us that was both spiritually uplifting and was happy and vibrant. A cloak had been spread over the area – a cloak of protection and of healing that our forefathers had experienced. Of course we were all thrilled at what we had been able to do but it was not just that sense of upliftment we were experiencing. It was much more.

I have long been of the opinion that Leek and its surrounding area is something special. I have looked before, in a previous book, at the healing aspects of the water that flowed from the site of the

Double Sunset where a stone circle was erected and where later a Church dedicated to St Edward was built. It was this water that, in all probability, gave its name to the town as "Lec" meaning stream ... or could it have been these healing waters where there was once a chapel dedicated to Our Lady at Ladydale? I wonder. (The name could also mean 'Stone' – a fascinating mystery.)

The Sanctuary

But there is another aspect of this Healing Town, the place where a devout Christian lady was bequeathing her rambling Victorian home as a Healing Sanctuary and where there live many people devoted to healing, each in their own way.

Why should the old Leek Urban District Council have chosen a sign of healing as its own logo?

The coat of arms of the old Leek Urban District Council showing two coiled serpents around the winged staff, a Caduceus.

Was it a coincidence, I wonder, that the old crest or coat of arms of the now defunct Leek U.D.C. was a Caduceus? It was changed to something less "mystical" in the 1950s, and I think I know why. Caduceus is Latin for a herald's staff of office associated with Hermes, the Greek god and it is also a symbol of healing. It is a wand or staff with two serpents or two snakes entwined around it and sometimes there are wings on the top of the staff. In alchemy it is used as the sign of uniting the opposites. The wand signifies power and the snakes depict wisdom. Snakes are also known as

Wyrms or Dragons or Serpents. Dragon lines and Serpent lines are a description of earth energy lines or power lines. In Christian terms, St Michael or St George are often shown as defeating the "dragon" or "serpent", the evil or "pagan" force ... and pagan means "of the earth". The Caduceus is also a symbol of sexual energy or power and was a prototype of the magic wand used by the magicians of today; the twin currents of the sun and the moon are shown as serpents twined about the pole and the breath of the wand and the equilibrium in balance – in Eastern religious theory and thinking the yin and the yang – passes its influence to the wand thus making it powerful enough to carry out the will of the magician. It is a very potent force in the minds of many and I believe this potent force was alive in the minds of the originators of the Leek crest.

Well of the Hermit Prince

There is a place where, according to one of the country's leading authorities on the paranormal, Paul Devereaux, "the earth spirit is close at hand." In his book co-written with Ian Thomson and called "The Ley Hunter's Companion" (Thames and Hudson 1979) this spiritual spot is at one of the outposts of Northern Staffordshire, the picturesque and haunting village of Ilam.

Ilam, it is said, is one of the southernmost villages on the Pennine Chain and its name is Saxon for "at the hills". The village, visited by countless thousands of tourists every year, is surrounded by Thorpe Cloud and two twin hills known as The Bunsters. On the other side is the magnificent wooded valley so aptly named Paradise, the area behind Ilam Hall that inspired Dr Johnson to write his novel "Rasselas" and where the English dramatist William Congreve wrote much of his play "The Old Bachelor". The neo-Gothic Hall was built in the early nineteenth century by industrialist Jesse Watts Russell and the ornate monument in the centre of the village was erected by him in memory of his wife.

It is a pleasant but tortuous journey to this village (demolished and rebuilt by Russell to give a better view from his mansion) and the immediate question about the place is why was it here? It is in the middle of nowhere and yet possesses a church old in Saxon times. The answer is that the area was a spot where pilgrims came to visit a prince of the royal household who became a holy man with healing powers and when he died the shrine erected to him was placed in a chapel that became a church – the present Church of the Holy Cross.

St Bertram's Well where, it has been written, the Earth Spirit remains.

So who was he? And why was he at this spot? "He" was Bertram, later to become a saint. His name is sometimes spelt as Bertelin and he was the son of a Prince of Mercia who travelled to Ireland, returned with a wife and suckling babe and on their way to Stafford his wife and child were devoured by wolves. He became a hermit at the site now known as Bertram's Well. That is it in a nutshell, but there is far more meat on the bone as I shall now tell. This, it is believed, is the same St Bertram or Bertelin who is the patron saint of Stafford, the town boasting his relics. Others would have it that it is a different person altogether.

The chronicler Capgrave tells that Bertram, the son of a Mercian King, lived in the eighth century and he fell in love with a princess while on a visit to Ireland. The same story is told in the "Dictionary of Saints" (Kay and Ward Ltd., 1982). Bertram brought his bride back from Ireland and, it is thought, landed at Chester. He was returning to his family home at Stafford according to the majority of stories, but I think the family home was at Tamworth, when his pregnant wife began to give birth and they had to stop in some woods. He went for a midwife, it is related, and when he returned discovered wolves had torn both his wife and newly born child to pieces. He was so beside himself with grief that he became a hermit, it is said.

Other learned treatises have it that he went to study under St Guthlac in the middle of the Lincolnshire Fens. Later, Bertram (or sometimes Bettelin, Beccelin and even Berthelm) was called to his master's deathbed and he "counselled Bertram with such wisdom that he never before or after heard the like". It is also said that Guthlac was financed by Aethelbald, King of Mercia and it is highly likely he was the father of the Hermit Prince Bertram. What the aged Holy Man told the young Bertram stayed with him all his life. He was probably told of the secrets of healing, secrets known to only a few and secrets that could only be extracted from the land itself. Hence his stay at Ilam in North Staffordshire.

Bertram stayed in an anchorite's cell somewhere, according to Capgrave, "near Stafford". Where this was we do not know and translation may account for it being "near Stafford" and not "in Stafford's Shire". In other words, he may have originally had an anchorite's cell near Stafford or may have been at Ilam from the outset. We do not know, but we do know he spent his final years in the north of the Shire. However, on the death of his father he had to forsake his hermit's life for a while to lead the royal army in "driving off an invader". A legend has it that he drove off this invader with the assistance of an angel "sent from Heaven to oppose the demon who led the opposing forces". Then Bertram returned to his cell, the chronicler states, and lived there for the rest of his days. This final sentence is telling in that it almost certainly places his cell at Ilam.

But why Ilam? It was certainly one of the furthest outposts of his father's empire but the spot where St Bertram's Well is situated is on one of the most powerful earth energy lines in the British Isles. According to "The Ley Hunter's Companion" this line is some sixteen and a quarter miles long, starting at Foolow in the High Peak of Derbyshire, going through Arbor Low and concluding at St Bertram's Well.

St Bertram's Well and the healing tree to the right.

This well is still to be found just north of the village of Ilam. From the ornate monument in the centre of the village follow the road along the riverbank for a few hundred yards and then, on the left hand side, notice a footpath that goes past Townend Farm. The well is situated on one of the hills known as Bunster, and is about a brisk five minutes walk along the footpath, skirting the drystone wall. When the traveller comes to this spot, he or she must immediately be aware of the enormous sense of peace and tranquillity that surrounds this area. This is the spot where our holy man lived and where pilgrims came to be healed by him. They came from all over the ancient kingdom of Mercia, and the path today is the same path trodden by their feet so many centuries before. Just above this well is a tree, a maple. It has grown on the self-same spot where an ash tree once grew (and some say, was chopped down in an act of Puritan zeal). This is a healing tree, just as the waters that come from the limestone-bedecked well are healing waters to this day. Sit under this tree, feel its trunk surround you as an arm cradling an infant child, and eat and breath its healing vibrations. This tree has been watered throughout its life by the healing stream that flows from the well. At one time in the history of the site the ash tree that grew there used to be bedecked with garlands and pilgrims nailed coins to its trunk. To this day there is a tradition that if anyone takes anything from the tree, a piece of bark or a twig, then harm will befall them. This tradition must go back many centuries and shows how the tree was venerated.

Even in the Middle Ages this area was a site for pilgrimages, and later the church itself at Ilam took over as the site to be venerated and worshipped. The tomb of St Bertram is splendidly displayed inside the ancient building and even to this day people come to the shrine to be healed.

When Hilary and I visited it in the autumn of 1993 people had left items in thanks to the Saint – flowers, a prayer book, words written on cards, and other personal objects. The Saint's healing powers did not die with him and even though his body is no longer at Ilam (it was moved to Stafford) his spirit remains.

Close by the Church there is another well, between the building and the river, dedicated to the Saint and it looks like this was a spot where people could be immersed in the waters, obviously in the hope of being healed. There is no earthly reason why this spot should be a healing spot. No earthly reason, but a holy and spiritual reason, yes. For if the pilgrim believes he or she will be healed by immersion in these waters then there is a good chance that something will happen. The mind is a very powerful healer.

There are some wondrous stone crosses or shafts in the grounds of the Church. These contain much energy. And all around this magical place there are signs that ancient man has thought the area something special. Ancient burial mounds abound and the rocks are powerful. The River Dove is the border of Staffordshire and Derbyshire at this point and the venerated river cascades around the village. Do visit here, you will take away more from this spot than you brought with you.

The tomb in Ilam Church. Even today, some thirteen hundred years or more after the Saint's death, people still give offerings to his tomb, in the hope of receiving healing.

69

More water magic

Just what magical and mysterious power does the water that flows from some of our local wells and springs contain? Not only does this water refresh (although I would recommend caution in sampling certain waters in this chemical age) but it most certainly does heal the mind and body. Perhaps some would argue that it is a healing of the troubled mind more than a healing of the sick body and I would neither agree nor disagree on this point for, as long as the cure works, I go along with that Hollywood hero who said, "Frankly, my dear, I don't give a damn." Belief in a cure is ninety per cent of the way towards a cure.

But the sites where some of these spots are situated hold a clue to the curative properties also. The Ladydale Well at Leek is on four very powerful earth lines and the water passes through them before spouting out. Does this alter the state of the water and make it something special? What is remarkable about this well is that it is connected by two different paths to another healing well some few miles away. From Ladydale there is a distinct path than can still be walked that goes to the Egg Well at Bradnop. Coupled with this is a distinct earth line that joins the two.

The waters of many springs and wells contain minerals they have picked up on their journey through the earth's crust.

Just outside Leek on the road to Ashbourne is the village of Bradnop and there can be found a well that used to be venerated for its healing properties and, indeed, still is. It is known as The Egg Well. Maybe this stems from the fact that it is more or less oval in shape but ancient Druidic lore often refers to eggs in connection with healing rites and the Celtic holy men believed the universe was hatched from two eggs. The stone basin of the Egg Well has a Latin inscription surrounding it which translated reads: "The liver, kidneys, heart's disease ... these waters remedy and by their healing powers assuage many a malady ..." Today the well is surrounded by a modern brick structure although within living memory it was surrounded by an ornate iron structure. Perhaps this went as a result of the War Effort, melting down anything that stood that was of iron. Don't drink of this water, I beg of you. It is now still and stagnant and is no longer a freshly running supply.

Staffordshire Healing Path

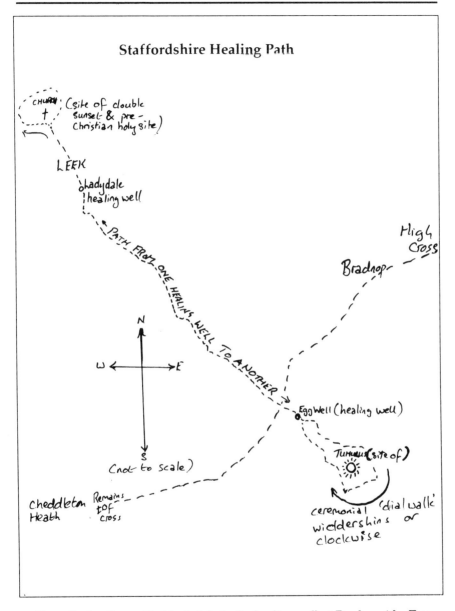

From the healing well at Ladydale to the healing well at Bradnop (the Egg Well) there is a footpath. Why should these two sites be joined if not for a ceremonial walk?

71

Interior and exterior of the Egg Well.

Somewhere or other the supply of healing water to this site has been severely restricted at one time and the well suffers for it. It is now itself in need of healing. Close by there is an area known as Lady Fields. A coincidence when you think that it is connected with Lady Dale and perhaps there was a Christianisation of the Earth Mother here as well; or perhaps the name is just a continuation of the remembrance of the healing Earth Mother. This is the area known locally as the place where the fairy folk meet.

And what about St Bertram's Well at Ilam? This is on one of the strongest earthlines in this country. Perhaps a coincidence and, then again, perhaps not.

Many wells, once renowned for their healing properties, have now been lost to us whether through neglect or deliberate suppression. There is, or was, a well known as Ladywell or Marian's Well at Uttoxeter. It is still on the Ordnance Survey map, shown as being in fields at the back of a row of houses that front the road out to Marchington. This well, it was once recorded, was where the ghost of a woman, said to be Maid Marian, haunted. This spirit was probably memories of the Water Goddess and the legend of the ghost could quite probably have been "invented" to keep people away ... people other than those who could use the healing properties to their own advantage. it did happen, there were crooks and tricksters then just as there are today.

At Church Eaton there is a well dedicated to St Edith; and here we have yet another example of the Church taking over a site of healing and worship and giving it a Christian name. It has happened not only throughout this county of ours but throughout all of Britain and all of Europe. Over the past few centuries it has happened on the Continents of America and Australia also.

Rushton Spencer

Then there is the well at Rushton Spencer that can tell the future ... or so it is said. I have mentioned this before in a previous work, but will make brief mention once more if you will allow. St Helen's Well lies just off the main road from Macclesfield to Leek. As the motorist approaches from Macclesfield the road takes a sharp right hand at the Royal Oak pub and many motorists now continue along the road "over the top" here, thus avoiding a wibbly wobbly route around Rudyard Lake. As this hilly short cut is taken, just to the right is where the well is situated. I am pleased to report that at the time of writing this well has been given a spring clean and it is looking very spruce; but for many years it had been neglected. This well, it is said, would suddenly dry up and whenever it did it foretold evil, the Rushton folk feared. The well ran dry before the Civil War when Charles I was beheaded; then there was the famine of 1670; the Gunpowder Plot; the outbreak of the First and Second World Wars; the deaths of monarchs ... all occasions when its fortune telling proved correct. Nowadays it seems to be permanently dry. I wonder what that means.

The Gruel Spout

At Biddulph there is another well the locals feel has special powers. It is called the Gruel Spout and to this day people will queue up to fill containers with its waters. Here, the ancient tradition of well dressing – or giving thanks to the Water Spirit or Goddess – has been revived. Today, the neighbouring County of Derbyshire has revived many well dressing ceremonies and, unfortunately, Staffordshire has lost many. They used to be held in The Black Country at Codsall, Monmore Green, Bilbrook and Brewood. Over at Endon, near to Leek, the well dressing ceremony is very much alive; one of the last places in Staffordshire where this tradition continues. Rushton people decided to stop their well dressing in the 1920s; perhaps one day they will revive it, who knows?

Waters of Wolverhampton

All towns and villages had wells, rivers or springs to water the population and some of these spots were used for healing in addition to refreshment. Take Wolverhampton, for instance; one of the most ancient of the southern towns of Staffordshire. This was Wulfrunes Heanton, the High Town of Wulfruna. This Wulfruna was the widow of Aldhelm, the Earl of Northampton and it was she who gave lands to the monastery at Heantun. In the 1686 book that has become a "bible" for Staffordshire historians, Plot's

"Staffordshire", there is a piece that reads: "Nor comes the town of Wolverhampton far behind Swynnerton, being situated high and where they have but four weak springs to supply that large town which, too, rise altogether behind the Cock Inn (so that they may be esteemed as one), having different names appropriated to their several uses as the Pudding Well, the Horse Well, the Washing Well and the Meat Well, from which they fetch all the water they use for meat or drink all over the town in great leather budgets, or boraccias, laid across a horse with a funnel at the top to fill them, such as they much use in Spain."

Chapel Ash at Wolverhampton, taken over 90 years ago. It has changed much since. This was where people came for healing waters many years ago.

But outside of Wolverhampton, there were other wells worthy of more attention. On the road out to Wednesfield there was the Cul Well, the head of the River Smestall, that was said never to dry up and where local people used to make offerings in the form of money and statues. There was a well renowned for its healing properties at Chapel Ash on the Dunstall Estate and now, alas, no more.

At Spring Vale in Wolverhampton is the site, or was the site, of the most powerful of all the area's healing waters. This was once known as Wulfruna's Well. Wulfruna was drawn to Wolverhampton for a variety of reasons and she gave, as we have seen, much of her wealth to the holy men of those parts. But why? Tradition has it that she often visited the well or the waters at Spring Vale that were named after her; she would bathe and she would drink the water. Obviously the lady derived benefit from this; and that benefit was undoubtedly healing. Some writers have quoted a sixteenth century document that said: "To ye south of Wolferhamptune ys a famous sprynge wher shee usyd to come and washe. Yt ys saide yt ye ladie prayede for yt God woude endue yt with powers of no ordinaire virtu, inasmuch as yt itt hathe curyd manie, as itt we myraculouslie, healynge ye lame, ye weake, ye infirme, as manie the bee can testyfie."

But Wolverhampton's miracle waters are not confined to these; there were more. Deepfields derives its name from Dip Fields and this signified the place where sick people were dipped into the water to be healed; it was also used later by the church for baptisms I understand – perhaps yet another indication of the church taking over a pre-Christian ceremony. Were people "baptised" with the waters of the Earth Goddess at this spot at one time, I wonder?

People have "taken the waters" at Spa Towns for countless centuries. These spa towns became fashionable again in the Georgian and Victorian eras but just before then, in the late 1600s, Lady Gerard of Gerard's Bromley discovered, or rather re-discovered, warm springs at Willoughbridge on the borders of Cheshire and Shropshire. She erected a bath house and tried to entice people there of take of the waters. Locals still maintain that the beneficial properties of the waters had been known to everyone except this lady up until then. It was only when she was let into the secret that the whole world was told.

But, returning to the ancient town of Wolverhampton ... on the way out to Walsall there stands the equally ancient market town of Willenhall. Today, it is built up, it has a legacy of brass and iron foundries and it is close by the motorway network but at one time there was an attempt to make this town into a Spa Town also. There was a well, as ancient as the town and as ancient as the land before the town was thought of; its waters contained much sulphur – the breath of the earth dragons – and for countless years people had flocked to it to drink and to bathe. Then in the early 1700s, certain local gentry tried to make this place into a spa. It almost succeeded, but the Industrial Revolution was taking place and there was far more money to be made from locks, keys and bolts being manufactured at the local foundries. The sulphurous waters were pretty soon rivalled by the far unhealthier sulphurous fumes emanating from the factories.

Just to the west of Wolverhampton there is the suburbanised area known as Codsall where more sulphurous water was, and is, to be found. In Codsall Wood there was the Leper House where people suffering from the disease went to bathe in the waters. And it was not just leprosy that the waters were thought to cure, all manner of skin complaints could be helped by bathing in these waters, it used to be thought.

In most of the towns and villages and parishes of Staffordshire, people derived benefit from the waters that came from out of the ground. In days now gone the land was purer, we had not started to poison that which gives us life; we venerated the land. We relied upon the land for our existence. Today we discard and kill the land. Such sadness.

There was also a well at Bilston, once dedicated to St Chad and later known as the well of St Crudley (whoever he or she was – most probably a derivation of 'Chad', I think) which not only was the main source of water for the town but also contained properties of a curative nature. The townsfolk must have been very healthy.

Burton upon Trent is now more famous for its ale than for its water; but that has not always been the case. Brewing appears to have been started by the monks of Burton Abbey in the Middle Ages. That illustrious Abbey stood on the banks of the Trent but it was not from that River they drew their water. No, they used water from the wells of Burton and these wells had long been known for their curative properties. There is a large amount of gypsum within this water drawn from under the town and the local people knew of this long before the monks decided it would make a nice pint or two of booze. This area is a spot well known to the Ancients. They were here not only for the healing waters but for the mystic qualities of the surrounding countryside as well, and buried their dead all around this area. Horninglow, now a suburb, is testimony to this as is Drakelowe on the other side of the river, where there is now a huge power station blotting the landscape for many miles around. The suffix "Lowe" indicates an ancient burial ground.

One well in particular at Burton was renowned throughout Mercia for its healing properties. Later, the Celtic Christian Saint called Modwen had her name appended to it. The well was at a site known as Andressy, perhaps a corruption of St Andrew's Isle, situated on the flat meadow across from the church, and there are a number of records relating how huge crowds used to visit the spot in the hope of receiving cures for illness. A building was erected over it and made into a place of worship but, no doubt, it had been a place of worship for many centuries before.

So many to choose from!

The list is never ending. At Mow Cop, where the folly stands on the rocky outcrop separating Staffordshire and Cheshire, there is still a spring which never dries up and, again, is looked upon as containing healing properties. Near to Newcastle under Lyme is Salters Well (no doubt the name indicating the use of it by the salters, packhorsemen or jaggers that went from Cheshire eastwards and southwards), and there was yet another Lady Well at Wombourn where a hermit used to reside. Here, no doubt, there were cures on offer from the Holy Man as well as from the waters, but I rather fancy the healing waters were what attracted the Hermit in the first place. This was dedicated later to the Virgin Mary but was, I wonder, Lady Well originally dedicated to the Earth Mother, or Lady, Brigit?

In the north there were sulphurous waters at Butterton and at Weston while at Willowbridge to the south of Newcastle the waters there were extremely lively, perhaps containing natural gases at one time. Over at Cheadle there was the well that was said to be able to cure many a malady. This was at Rockcliffe where the water cascaded from the side of the hill and besides its medicinal properties it, like the well at Rushton, was used to predict the future. This particular well foresaw events by the amount of bubbles on its surface when someone threw stones or other objects into it; rather like the bones used by witch doctors or the runes cast by ancient man. It is recorded that there used to be stones surrounding this well with inscriptions upon them but they were removed to be used in buildings. There was a similar healing well at Huntley, close by.

Many springs were thought to give healing water. Here, members of Leek Rambling Club pause for a drink at Flash in the early 1930s. Judging by the snow on the ground that water must have been quite cool! (Mr and Mrs Pace).

Another well taken over in later times by the church was St John's Well at Shenstone and what used to be known as the Elder Well or the Wise Well at Blymhill later became known as St Mary's Well.

Near to Tamworth is Canwell, said to receive its name from "Well of Power" and where Benedictine monks took over the powerful earth energy and built a monastery. They gave the well over to St Modwen, as at Burton. Divining rods in my hands showed there was, indeed, a very strong earth line at the spot and Hilary, my wife, whose mediumistic powers I have talked about before, substantiated the fact that people had gained more than healing from this spot. They had received mental and physical stimulation. Perhaps, then, it was no coincidence that these waters were said to be beneficial for nervous disorders.

But we cannot leave this look at the Healing Waters of Staffordshire without taking a journey of pilgrimage to St Chad's Well at Lichfield. Elsewhere in this book we look at Lichfield, the mystical centre of England and the early Christian Saint Chad who was said to be responsible for the place. St Chad's Well is, quite obviously, dedicated to this man.

A historian called Leland, who lived between 1506 and 1552 wrote: "Stowe Church, in the east end of the town, where is St Chadd's Well, a spring of pure water. where is seen a stone in the bottom of it, on which, some saye, St Chadd was wont, naked, to stand in the water and praye. At this time St Chadd had his oratory in the tyme of Wulphan, King of the Merches" (Mercia). St Chad was to become the Patron Saint of medicinal springs.

It was from these waters that the Saint baptised converts to the Christian faith; and in those days there were many thousands upon thousands of the Mercian Kings dictated that the one and only religion was to be that of Christ. The people had no alternative than to comply, and the followers of Woden and of Brigit became followers of Jesus. At least on the surface.

The waters from this well were said to cure sore eyes and over the centuries countless numbers have visited this site for the healing properties and for the religious significance the well has. There have been a number of edifices placed over it over the years, during the reign of the Stuarts something looking like a temple was built over it and Charles the Second's physician, John Floyer, built a bath house nearby to which people flocked to the immersed in the cold waters.

Throughout the country there are, now, wells and springs dedicated to St Chad and, at Lichfield, it is still possible to receive a cure by visiting the Holy Place. If you believe.

Rushton well dressing festival, 1912. Sir Philip and Lady Brocklehurst are in the centre.

5

Staffordshire Superstitions

The Wise People

The very existence of superstitions implies that people believe there is a power beyond themselves that must be bribed by action or deed and won over or, perhaps, encouraged to go away.

Here in Staffordshire there have been many superstitions practised over the centuries and many still are. The Horn Dance at Abbotts Bromley is a manifestation of an ancient superstition that if a ritual was not enacted then ill-luck and infertility would fall on the community. Whenever a flint arrowhead was uncovered, usually near an ancient burial mound often called a Fairy Hill, these arrowheads had to be embedded in a tree, to give them back to their owners – the fairy people.

Whatever the ritual, from crossing fingers when walking under ladders to knocking on wood (to appease the tree spirits), they have survived the ages. Some of us still carry charms, perhaps in the form of religious items like a cross on a chain or a "lucky" charm that could be a coin, a rabbit's foot or whatever. Not so very long ago stones from The Roaches were carved into amulets to ward off the Evil Eye and many North Staffordshire people wore Roaches Millstone grit around their necks. Some still do.

Many Staffordshire superstitions were brought to light by the Reverend E. Deavon who gave an address to the North Staffs Field Club in 1930. In it he told that in the Potteries, people who saw a parson with a round hat on would touch a piece of iron before passing him. Any old bit of iron would do, apparently, a gas pipe or railings or somesuch. He said that the superstition of touching wood meant touching wood of the cross, but on this I must disagree with him. As I have said before, it is to do with the tree spirits in my opinion. And he elaborated that the custom of touching iron was meant to be the touching of the nails of the cross. Perhaps he is correct on this.

The Reverend Gentleman was in charge of parishes within the Weaver Hills, a North Staffordshire area abounding in ancient history. He told of an old woman who had brought up a family of eleven boys and girls in a three roomed house. He said that had she lived some three or four hundred years ago she would have been burned at the stake as a witch because she had cures for many ailments. This was by no means uncommon in rural communities, every area had a healer of some description. Anyway, this particular lady had two cures for whooping cough. One was the Lord's Prayer written backwards, sewn up in a piece of linen or silk and worn around the neck. The second was one that she used on her grandson after the doctors had all given him up and it saved his life – a mouse fried in butter and given to the patient.

A Staffordshire cure for measles was to cut some hair from the exact centre of the cross on a donkey's back, tie it up in a little linen bag and suspend it around the sufferer's neck.

It was believed that sacrament wine was a certain cure for a child who was wasting away and for whom the doctors could do nothing. Another Staffordshire custom was to take the child suffering from whooping cough outside and let he or she look at the new moon, rubbing a right hand up and down the child's stomach, looking steadfastly at the new moon and repeating: "What I see may it increase. What I feel may it decrease. In the name of the Father, Son and Holy Ghost, Amen."

For Thrush or "Frog", as it is sometimes referred to in Staffordshire, a remedy was supposedly to catch a baby frog, tie a piece of string to its hind leg and let the infant suck it instead of a dummy.

Staffordshire people thought a toad would spit poison. It doesn't, of course, but I wonder if this particular superstition goes back to the mists of time – like so many do – when toads living in these isles really were poisonous and it has survived in this way. There are poisonous toads in other parts of the world but thankfully not here in Staffordshire any more.

And then there is the Evil Eye. It has not only been the rural communities that have feared the Evil Eye, for town and city folk have long been plagued by this fear as well. It has been used as a form of blackmail by many wicked people, for the superstitious would eagerly buy off a supposed Witch or follower of the Black Arts in exchange for them not giving the Evil Eye to their livestock or, indeed, themselves. In Quarnford a family had to move away because their livestock had been given the Evil Eye as they thought.

The Reverend Deacon told his listeners at the North Staffs Field Club that in a row of cottages two babies were born within about a week of each other. One mother got up and about again and went out without being "churched" – being visited by a priest – and as she went out she looked at the other mother's house. The baby died and the second mother was quite prepared for this.

If a man lost a pig or met with any other misfortune then he believed he had been bewitched. As we have seen, it was often the case that someone would have told him that the Evil Eye was being placed on him. He had to pay up or suffer the consequences but there was another way out for the luckless person. He or she could visit a Wise Woman and have the curse removed.

What was meant as a Wise Woman? We have already heard about the woman of the Weaver Hills who had her own cures for ailments and that is just what a Wise Woman used to be (and, I must add, still is). Every community had a person, most commonly an elderly woman but it could have been a man as well, who would be conversant with the ancient ways of healing. Herbs from the fields and woodlands, waters from the springs and incantations from the mists of time were all utilised by these people, often with very startling results. The more isolated the community then the more reliant those people would be on their Wise Woman. If a woman was in childbirth then there was always the Wise Woman to assist. If someone was on their deathbed and all attempts at healing had failed then their journey to the next life was made easier by potions and concoctions put together by the Wise Woman.

The North Staffordshire Weaver Hills are akin to the North Staffordshire Roaches and in these ancient high rocks there used to be a thriving community isolated by the weather and by geography. Visits by doctors were few and far between and there had to be, over the centuries, a number of these Wise People – people wise about the healing arts. One such was Hannah Pickford, an ancestor or mine, who lived at Blue Hills Farm for many years.

A great, great Aunt of mine, Hannah Pickford of The Blue Hills on the Roaches. Later, she was at "Hannah's Buildings". She was known locally for the healing she was able to give, through herbs and potions and the knowledge handed down to her. She would be called, in some parts, a Wise Woman.

Hannah was often called upon to aid sick people which she gladly did. She was a woman wise in the ways of healing and her healing skills are still utilised within my family, I am pleased to say. She, and people like her, were often called upon to heal the troubled mind as well, for if a superstitious person believed the Evil Eye had been placed on them then it was up to people like Hannah to make them believe otherwise. Such was the belief in the capabilities of the Wise Ones that the giving of a charm was sufficient to ward off the Evil Eye, or perhaps the recital of a piece from the Bible would do the trick. The power of the mind is a very great power.

Charms for witches

A good number of years ago, Elijah Cope wrote about what he termed "witchraft" in the moorlands. He said that charms of various kinds were in use by inhabitants of the moorlands "and are not altogether discontinued at the present time" (this being about the middle of the eighteenth century). Their nature and use were various. Bits of brass, copper, lead and other material, with strange letters engraved upon them were placed upon churns to make the butter come quicker and more plentiful; on the plough to enable one horse to do the work of two; on the flail to enable the thresher to do more and better work. There were family charms which were put on when going on a journey as protection against accidents. Love charms in abundance which girls wore to draw to them the youths to love them.

Some of these were nothing more than a piece of paper with the youth's name written on it, worn near the heart. The girl who had been jilted gathered twelve smooth stones which she threw into a pool of water one at a time, calling the faithless lover's name as a means of bringing him back to her. Some old women of the area added to their income by selling secret charms to young people of both sexes by which they would compel friend or sweetheart to come to them.

The writer went on that a North Staffordshire farmer of great age had told him that his father had travelled, mostly on foot, to Oxford to purchase a bee, which is a kind of talisman, to enable him to dispense with any hired help on his farm. A bee, he explained, is a small bit of parchment about two inches by one in size and some words, unknown to anyone but the vendor were written on it. It was fastened to the heel of the scythe to enable the mower to do the work of many men. By some it was fastened to the plough by means of a bit of string. He wrote that many people had most implicit faith in their bee as a talisman.

He gave further insight into the superstitions of the area as well. If a farmer bought a cow at a market or from a neighbour and while taking it home a magpie flew over its back the cow was sure to die. If a cow or horse was ill and a bran mash was given to it the mash should not be mixed with a sharp instrument or that animal would die. Some housewives will not, he wrote, on any account whilst sweeping the floors brush anything towards the door as that would be sweeping good luck out of the house. Others will not sweep from the door inwards as that would be sweeping bad luck in.

At Wednesbury, people dreaded a burning cinder falling out of the fireplace. This cinder was called a "coffin" for it was thought to mean a death would occur. Another harbinger of death was if a marble rolled down a staircase it meant a young person would die.

The white cattle

There is a very famous story concerning a superstition surrounding a herd of white cattle. In the reign of Henry III, William Ferrers became the Earl of Derby and was given Chartley Castle after he married the sister of Randle, Earl of Chester. It is thought that it was William Ferrers who first enclosed in this great park some of the ancient white cattle that had been roaming Needwood Forest for centuries. From the thirteenth century through to the beginning of the twentieth century these cattle retained the purity of breed having white bodies with black ears, muzzles and hoofs. Sickness saw their demise, however. The superstition surrounding them is that a black calf was born to the herd when Earl Ferrers led the disastrous rebellion against the King and the family's downfall ensued. Whenever a black or blemished calf was born to the herd after this it meant the death of a member of the Ferrers family.

The White Chartley Cattle. A tradition surrounding them told of ill-fortune falling on their owners if a black calf was born.

There are a great number of superstitions or beliefs about Good Friday. No washing must be done on that day and certainly no soap-suds can be thrown out. Good luck will be brought if any item of metal is found on that day, again this could be the belief of touching iron because of the iron nails in the cross. If it rains heavily then the rainwater should be collected as, it was believed, it can be used for skin complaints and distress of the eyes. Styes in the eyes were cured by rubbing them with the tip off the tail of a black tom cat. Cats were supposed to have healing properties. In Staffordshire warts used to be cured by rubbing them night and morning with the tail of a tortoiseshell tom cat in the month of May. The blood taken from a black cat's tail and smeared on the part affected was thought to cure shingles. This complaint was believed to have been a kind of coiling snake and if the head and tail met then the patient would die.

Warts would disappear, it was said, if rubbed by a dead man's hand. There were, and there still are, people known as wart charmers. The North Staffs Field Club was told of one who was known very well and he would make a few passes with his hand over the warts and next morning they would have gone.

It was a fairly general custom to stand a poker on end in front of a fire that was burning badly. The poker in front of the bars of the grate would therefore make a cross. It was believed the fire was drawing badly because some ill-natured devils were sitting on top of the chimney and stopping the draughts. When they looked down the chimney and saw the cross they would fly away.

No-one would pick wood anemones called The Death Bloom much planted in graveyards. Staffordshire people would run past a group growing for they thought the air was tainted with death.

No-one would burn elder wood for there was a legend that the cross was made from elder. It is also supposed to be immune to lightning.

There used to be many well dressings within Staffordshire but now they are mainly confined to neighbouring Derbyshire. There was one at Rushton until the 1920s, as I have mentioned in a previous book. I had the pleasure of speaking to the last of the Well Dressing Queens, the former Miss Mary Eardley, who was crowned in 1924. St Helen's Well is just a short way up the hill from the Royal Oak and the local superstition was that if ever this well dried up then some disaster would occur. There is a well dressing ceremony still in existence at nearby Endon. I am pleased to say, and the thanksgiving to the water goddess has now been replaced by a Christian ceremony. The good people of Marston also thanked their water spirits in this way.

Many people in Staffordshire still believe that to bring may blossom into the house is unlucky. Wood felled when the moon is full will burn brightly, felled at another time it will not. A farmer near the Potteries is reported to have said he knew a particular winter would be a mild one because the leaves stayed on the trees for a long time whereas the year before he foretold an exceptionally severe winter because the leaves fell off early.

Some two thousand or more years ago, our ancestors were buried with food and drink to help them on their journey to the next life and in the Potteries only some fifty years ago there was a burial ceremony at which a man was given a Christian burial and in the coffin was a bottle of Bass and a loaf ...

Going a-souling

At Stanton on All Souls Eve the children would go around the village singing and expecting to be paid. According to an old book called "Popular Antiquities" the poor people of Staffordshire would go a-souling, begging or "puling" meaning "singing small" for soul cakes or, as the song said, "any good thing to make them all merry". The Folk Lore Society recorded on paper a souling song at Keele in 1880. It went:

Soul, soul, for an apple or two,
If you've got no apples, pears'll do.
Up with your kettles and down with your pans,
Pray, good Missis, a Soul Cake!
Peter stands at yonder gate
Waiting for a Soul Cake
One for Peter, two for Paul,
Three for Him who made us all.
Souling-day comes once a year -
That's the reason we come here!

The Soul Cake was specially made to be given to those who went a-souling. This is perhaps a survival of a dole of bread given to the poor on All Souls Day after the Requiem Mass and has degenerated into children singing for coppers.

All Souls Day commemorated the departed, and is a throw-back to the traditions of the souls of the dead roaming the earth on that night. We still have Halloween traditions and there has been a big revival in children begging during the night of All Hallows Eve, but it is now called Trick or Treat.

Throughout the Black Country, Bite Apple Day was celebrated. A game known as Bite Apple was played at Bilston and at Wednesbury and surrounding areas and this day was dedicated to St Clement. The old church at West Bromwich is dedicated to him. A similar game is still played throughout the country at Halloween, with an apple tied to a piece of string and suspended; the competitor trying to bite the apple without using his or her hands. A variation was to have a lighted candle attached and the participant could often get burnt.

At Christmas, lads of Staffordshire villages would black their faces and dress up and go round and ask permission to act out a small play at various houses. This was a survival of the Mummers Play still alive in neighbouring Cheshire. At Stanton they used to say they were going Guising – a verb to dress up as a disguised person – a Mummer. There was also the custom of wassailing – at Lichfield, for instance, there was a long established custom whereby Christmas revellers would knock on doors and ask the householder for "wassail" money to be placed in their cup. If not money, a drink would do. The word derives from the Anglo Saxon "hael" meaning to be of good health. Many of us still say "Good Health" when drinking a toast.

There was a custom at both Stanton and at Ipstones where after a wedding the bride and bridegroom on leaving the church would find their way barred. Across the road was stretched a rope held at both ends and the groom had to distribute largesse before being allowed to pass. The Reverend Deacon thought this might go back to the time when a man had to fight for a bride and the obstacles placed in his path represented the fight. The bride is offered the left arm of the groom at weddings – to keep his fighting arm free.

6

The UFO Window

Fear of the unknown

What is it about lights in the sky or mysterious shapes hovering overhead that not only intrigue but terrify as well?

The fear of the unknown has obviously a great deal to do with it, and since the first modern-day "scare" about Unidentified Flying Objects" in 1947 until the present day there has been not only a steady trickle of "sightings" but there has been a veritable flood of such occurrences.

Perhaps these unidentified objects in the sky are a purely natural phenomena. An author and journalist, Dave Clarke, who is a very good friend of mine, has suggested (and so have others) that these Earthlights as they are sometimes termed are perhaps completely natural. The quarry workings in the Peak District are a very good place to witness these purely natural phenomena.

And then there is Jenny Randles, probably one of the world's foremost authorities on the U.F.O. phenomena, who keeps a very open mind. She told me that ninety five per cent of reported sightings can be explained quite rationally. It is the other five per cent that are interesting, but perhaps they, also, will be explained one day. Over the years, as a journalist and writer, I have met many people who have seen "something" in the sky. I am certain they have all witnessed something strange. Just what, however, is perhaps a matter that time alone may tell ... or then again it will not.

I, too, have endeavoured to keep an open mind on the subject but I have to say that, having seen an object in the sky that could not be identified, then I am prepared to believe that the subject is certainly worthy of attention.

In 1979 or 1980, I cannot say which because of the inadequacy of my memory, I and my two sons saw a golden ball, stationary in the sky, above Rudyard in North Staffordshire. What is was I shall never be able to say. My eldest son, Robin, called me to the porch of our house at Rudyard one Sunday afternoon shouting "Dad, there's a space ship!" There was certainly a glowing object, gold and shimmering, stationary in the clear blue sky. It stayed in that position for some five minutes before disappearing in a southerly direction at an enormous speed. And that was that. Our one and only "sighting" if sighting it was. The sad and sorry point about it all was that there was a camera in the hallway not a couple of strides away but so fascinated was I by whatever this object was that I did not think to photograph it. How I have chastised myself about this since! However, there was a report that a lady in Leek had seen the same, or a similar, object, at the same spot. I received, many years later, a letter from a lady then living in Congleton who had seen an object hovering over Rudyard Lake and then shooting off at a great speed; and a middle-aged couple from Norton in the Moors told me that they had seen a similar U.F.O. back in the early seventies as they were driving over the Earlsway past The Bridestones and the Fox Hotel, only a mile or so away from Rudyard.

In March of 1994, I had the pleasure of chairing a meeting at which Jenny Randles gave a lecture and during this she mentioned the case of a couple from North Staffordshire who genuinely believed they had been "abducted" by aliens. They were driving from Werrington when they noticed strange lights and their car engine gave out. The next thing they knew it was an hour later and they were just outside Ipstones. Then it was an hour after that and they were near to Macclesfield. Perhaps Jenny will write the full story when she has investigated further.

There is no doubt whatsoever that the area of North Staffordshire from Leek down to the Potteries and Stafford and, most probably, as south as Cannock Chase, is rich in stories of unidentified phenomena. Why this should be what is termed a "Window" for sightings is yet to be explained; but one theory is that the enormous amount of coal-mining and quarrying for the earth's minerals has something to do with disturbing the earth's crust to such an extent that sparks of earth energy (perhaps Earthlights) are occasionally given off. Another theory is that the land is so criss-crossed with earth energy lines or dragon lines or ley lines that these are a draw for alien spacecraft. I shall leave you to decide or to find your own theories.

Encounter with lights

I have found that certain types of people are more apt to witness the U.F.O. phenomena than others. People who have a strong psychic energy and also young people, especially teenagers, are high on the list. I have written before about a Medium who had a strange encounter with bright lights whilst she was in a car just by the Staffordshire and Cheshire borders. I have spoken to a gentleman from Knypersley in North Staffordshire who has seen strange lights in the sky on many occasions. He is not saying they are aliens from outer space and does not wish his name to be made public but he is saying that they were lights that could not be explained.

And, I have found, there are many people who have seen these lights or objects who have never reported them. They have not told the police, and most certainly have not told the media for fear of being ridiculed. I have spoken to countless numbers, especially since they know that I shall not divulge their names, who have had weird and wonderful experiences. They come from all walks of life, from bank managers and housewives to University graduates, retired people and devout churchgoers. The list is endless but they have all seen something. I know there are "cranks" as well who claim all manner of happenings to them and communication with Zog from Venus or Mars, but after over thirty years as a journalist I can separate the wheat from the chaff in most instances.

Undoubtedly the most publicised and least explained occurrence in the northern part of Staffordshire was at a housing estate at Bentilee in the Potteries back in the mid-1960s. Not only did countless people from the huge corporation estate see strange objects in the sky but many actually saw these objects land ... and scorch marks were left on the ground afterwards. Could anything up to one hundred people collectively be hallucinating at one time? Perhaps some learned psychiatrist or other could persuade me that it was possible, but could he or she persuade those many good people who actually saw whatever it was they did see? I doubt it. And, if it was collective hallucination, then how could that phenomena be explained? Why should, and how could, so many people see the same hallucination at the same time? True, there have been instances of holy visions recorded whereby crowds of many hundreds have seen the appearance of the Blessed Virgin, but usually these devout people have been there collectively to witness such a miracle anyway. In Stoke upon Trent on that day in the year 1967 there were several different reports of landings and many different people living within a radius of two or three miles all gave identical descriptions yet in most instances these people had never met, they were not in the same spot and they were unaware that anyone else had witnessed what they saw. There were identical descriptions of scorch marks on the ground and all in all there were upwards of eighty people who actually claim to have seen unidentified objects flying in the sky.

There is no point in me even attempting to explain this away, for I have not the faintest idea what went on that day. I do believe the vast majority of the residents of Bentilee did see something strange and out of the ordinary. I have certainly spoken to one or two of them and have found them to be genuine in their recounting of the tale for, not surprisingly, it is vividly etched in their memories forever.

And the list of sightings throughout this "window" on various times and dates is unending.

As I write this, it was a matter of a couple of days previously that I spoke to a couple who told me that some fifteen years previously – that would make it about 1980 or so – when they were courting, they were in their car at Red Street Park at Talke one night when they saw a massive orange and blue light hover above their car. The boyfriend got out of the car and it began to move slowly away and then moved forward again. He jumped back in to the vehicle and locked all the doors and they saw it was still there, some five or six feet above them, so they drove off. It was only when they told their family, later, that his brother mentioned he had seen something hovering over the top of his house and he had telephoned the police and alerted the neighbours. And then there was a couple in 1992 who saw a huge light descend onto the middle of the road at Clayton and they rang Keele University who were unable to help with an explanation.

And so it goes. On and on, the list is never ending.

I was asked to give a talk to the North Staffs Hospital Radio and the charming lady I spoke to over the telephone to arrange the date on which I was to go into the studio had no hesitation in telling me how she had retired to bed one evening when all of a sudden the entire room was lit up; she went to the window and saw a huge object in the sky, it was round at the front and was travelling past the window. She shouted her husband who came to look and they both noticed that, as it passed, the rear of the object was shaped like a cigar; completely different from the front. What could it have been? Its orange and silver lighting and its huge size certainly discounted it being any sort of air vehicle that we know of.

Then there was the chat I had with the D.J. from B.B.C. Radio Stoke ... I had gone to the radio station to record a regular spot I had been doing about myths and legends and all manner of strange happenings and found that the usual presenter, Kate Tebby, had to go to Tatton Park to record an interview so I was met by a very friendly young man who hosted the early morning show. As we were travelling up in the lift towards the studio, our conversation turned to Unidentified Flying Objects (not all that an unusual occurrence for me) and he said that he had seen one on his way into work one morning and had mentioned it over the airwaves. The telephone lines to that popular radio station were even more jammed than usual after that with people throughout the station's broadcasting area phoning in to report that they, too, had seen something rather strange in the sky. Often, I find, people are relieved to discover that it is not only they who have witnessed (or thought they witnessed) something odd. It is a great load off their minds to suddenly become aware that their brain has not been playing tricks because other people have seen the same thing as well.

I am willing to bet that wherever a group of people come together, be it at a party or be it at a place of work or wherever, if the conversation came around to witnessing strange phenomena in the skies then there would be at least one person in that group who would admit to having seen something or other. Sadly, however, there would be another who would think it a great laugh and would most probably pontificate that anyone who saw flying saucers with little green men inside them would most definitely be a raving loony, a hippy, or a candidate for the funny farm. Yet few, if any, see saucer-shaped objects and even fewer than that see little green men or men of any shape, size or colour at all. What they do see is a variety of odd shapes or lights in the sky. Nothing more and nothing less. And only a handful of the many hundreds of eye witnesses are brave enough to relate their experience, most probably through fear of ridicule.

I have looked into many reports of sightings in the skies over North Staffordshire over the years, but it would have been impossible for me to have got anywhere near to as many as that great Potteries institution and fine newspaper, the *Evening Sentinel*. This paper, the "bible" for North Staffordshire, has been chronicling events for countless years and no reports of unidentified flying objects in the skies above the Potteries and surrounding areas has ever escaped its net.

I knew that no discussion within these pages would be complete without consulting this "oracle" and so a phone call to a very obliging news room soon had me talking to Andy Hopwood who is responsible for the newspaper cuttings. I am indebted to him for allowing me to spend some time pouring over the cuttings that have appeared over the years and, although I was aware that there had been many sightings over the North Staffordshire area over the years, I was not aware of just how many. There are hundreds, and it would be impossible for me to give them all within these pages, but perhaps I can mention a small cross section, thanks to the good offices of the *Sentinel*.

The most recent one I came across was in January of 1994 when a motorist reported bright red and blue lights over the M6 motorway.

As if to support the fact that there were countless sightings over the area, a cutting for July 20th, 1990, said that reports had soared over the previous twelve months and officials at the U.F.O. Studies Centre in Earle Street, Crewe, had received 120 calls and most concerned mysterious lights over the Stoke-on-Trent and Stafford areas.

But most of the reports seemed to have been during the 1970s. On February 8th, 1977, for instance, the *Sentinel* told about the sighting of a U.F.O. by four Stafford policemen and a picture was published of an object taken by a County policeman on night patrol in 1971. He had snapped it with a patrol car camera.

In September of 1978 there was the story of how a U.F.O. had buzzed over a car whose occupants were a North Staffs couple. They saw a huge dark object pass overhead as they travelled through Dilhorne and it fired a blinding beam of light at their car. The driver, a 20 years old engineer from Trent Vale, said it was about 1.30 a.m. as he and his girlfriend were travelling home. They saw two lights, one red and one white, moving across the sky then out of nowhere an enormous black object loomed up in front of his car and shot a beam of light across them. There were two friends of theirs in a car in front and they also witnessed the event.

Tranter Road, Abbey Hulton, where several people saw unidentified flying objects.

There are many more reports of strange sightings in the area, but I shall confine my journey through the *Sentinel* files to just one more: in July of 1980 the newspaper reported that shocked householders at Abbey Hulton had seen a mysterious object in the sky. At least seven residents from the Tranter Road area spotted an object hovering over their rooftops. A teenage boy, then 16, called the police. His mother and her husband also witnessed it and she said it came from the Hanley direction and slowly passed overhead before disappearing over Birches Head. It was quite a large object, oval-shaped, and was a red or orange colour and it could be heard humming. Two teenage girls said it was moving slowly across the sky before it swooped down and rose again.

Then, of course, a North Staffordshire "happening" hit the national and international headlines when various eye witnesses reported seeing an R.A.F. Phantom jet shadowing an unidentified flying object over Newcastle. This was denied by the authorities at the time, I remember.

But the sightings are not confined to Stoke-on-Trent, for further south at Stafford – but most probably still in this "window" – there was the famous case of the County ambulance men who saw a strange U.F.O. from their headquarter windows.

The list goes on and on. I tuned in to satellite television recently to see a re-run of Arthur C. Clarke's *Mysteries* programme and there was a lady who used to live near to Stafford recounting her experience with a U.F.O. that had hovered over her farmhouse.

All these reported sightings have occurred where there are geological faults, either through the workings of man with mining operations or quarrying or through the workings of Mother Nature. This may be a complete and utter coincidence, or then again it may be looked upon as a rational explanation but I do feel that while we are dealing with such a diverse number of varying reports of completely different phenomena then an open mind should be kept.

An untold tale

But finally, before we go on to investigate other strange and mysterious aspects of wonderful Staffordshire, I must relate one incident that is stranger than fiction and is, so I am informed, completely and utterly true. I shall tell the tale as I was told it, and will refrain from comment, leaving you to make up your own mind.

This strange encounter was related to me by an eminent businessman who resides in North Staffordshire; I cannot divulge his name because, like so many people who have witnessed odd events, they are unwilling to be held to ridicule. He had only told his wife and his eldest son this story until he decided that I should be told. I have known him for some fifteen years and can vouch that he has always been level headed and astute and is very well educated. He tells me he does not believe in visitors from outer space and is sceptical about all aspects of earth mysteries and phenomena that I write about. So be it. This is what he told me.

On June 16th, 1991, our businessman – I shall call him Bill although that is not his real name – was driving to his North Staffordshire home from Chester at about 1.30 a.m. He decided to take what he termed a "short cut" through Congleton and then over the road from Congleton to the back of Rudyard and Rushton. (I have already mentioned a couple from Norton who saw an unidentified object along this road but several years previously.)

His business duties in Chester had necessitated him drinking many cups of tea, because his colleagues were all drinking alcohol but he had to refrain because he was driving home that night. However, as he was driving along the road to Rushton from Congleton he found that the copious cups of tea were taking their toll and he desperately needed to spend a penny. There was little or no traffic about and so he pulled up by the grass and hedgerow at the side of the road and went to the side of the car to do the necessary. As he was standing there he looked over towards The Bridestones, the neolithic burial chamber that is situated just off the roadway. The night was clear and, being close to midsummer, was not dark at all. The sky looked almost blue, he told me, and the two upright stones of The Bridestones could be easily distinguished. Bill had never, been to the Bridestones, he had no interest in them, but was aware of their existence and had passed them on countless occasions. He remembered thinking to himself that perhaps he would take a look at them one day and began to walk around to the driver's door after he had finished what he went out of the car to do.

It was then that he thought he saw someone with what he termed "a big spotlight" shining on The Bridestones. They became illuminated and in the light of the torch or whatever it was they looked a golden colour. He stopped and noticed that the entire area was illuminated. "That must be some spotlight" he thought to himself and a few seconds later the entire area seemed to give off "sparks" like static electricity. But these sparks were also golden in colour and he wondered if someone was having a party and letting off fireworks. Bill was in two minds whether to investigate or not, for he knew the Bridestones were protected as an Ancient Monument, but he thought better of it. He was alone, and did not know how many people in whatever state of intoxication he might encounter, so he got in the driver's seat and turned the ignition key to drive away. But his car would not start. He tried again and it would not respond, so he got out to have a look under the bonnet ... not that it would have done any good, he admitted to me, because he knew little or nothing about engines. As he got out of the car the light from The Bridestones rose above the Ancient Monument and began to glide towards him.

He stood, motionless, watching the golden ball glide towards him. He could not move, whether from fear or from any external force he could not say. He wanted to run but his legs would not let him. The golden object came over his head and he was aware of a huge pain behind his eyes – he later put it down to the enormous glow of the object – and thought he must have then passed out for he can remember nothing but what he described as "an empty darkness". There was no pain, there was no anything. He knows nothing of what happened after that until he came to, lying on the ground in the middle of a copse of trees some 200 metres or so away from where his car was. He was, not surprisingly, completely disorientated. He had no idea where he was but immediately recalled the bright golden light and his first instinct was to hide.

He told me: "I scrambled along on all fours, scratching myself on some brambles, and hid behind a silver birch tree. I eventually plucked up enough courage to peer around the trunk and could see nothing. I realised I was not wearing a shirt, just trousers, and my shoes were missing. What in heaven's name had happened to me?

I stood up and, for some reason, brushed my trousers and noticed that sparks were flying off them like static electricity. I walked to the edge of the copse and to a road, and walked along it for a short while and noticed my car at the same spot that I had left it. I began to run towards it, tripping over and scraping my elbow in the process. As I got near to it I saw a little bundle in the road. It was my shirt and underneath were my shoes. I put my shirt on, and put my feet into the shoes, which I noticed were unusually warm. I opened the car door – it was not locked – and saw my keys were in the ignition. I turned them, praying as I did so, and the car started first time. I must have reached sixty miles per hour in the space of a few feet. I was so anxious to get away. As I sped along that road I looked at the clock on the dashboard. It was about five minutes past three."

The copse where the mysterious "abduction" of the businessman concluded.

When he got home he told his wife he had been in an accident and it was only days later that he told her what he had experienced. "She did not believe me at first" he told me. "And I don't know whether she believes me now."

He has not reported it to any authorities and tells me he has no intention of ever doing so. I have been sworn never to divulge his identity and whereas I realise this lessens the impact of the story am offering it to you just as I was told it, without any additions or subtractions and without any comments.

7

The Highlands

Biddle Muir, Saracens and the Fairie Folk

Biddulph Moor is now a sprawling residential area that has joined hands with the nearby town of Biddulph and married into an urban conurbation but until relatively recently it was a place occupied by a hardy breed of dark-skinned people keeping themselves to themselves, a place where the inhabitants were said to speak a language other than that native to our land and where, tradition had it, descendants of a race of Saracens or Phoenicians still survived. There was and still is another tradition hanging broodily over that once bleak and desolate area; a memory of something only to be whispered about. A memory of the Good People, the Brownies, the Little People or, as we would have it today, the Fairie Folk. As we unravel these mysteries and lift the fog to, hopefully, let the sunlight shine through then these traditions and tales will intertwine to give a much clearer picture.

There has been a verbal tradition for many years of this unusual race of beings inhabiting the Biddulph Moorland and said to be descended from Saracens brought over during the Crusades. These dark skinned and dark haired people kept themselves very much to themselves, it was said. Local people have, most definitely, always looked upon the original occupants of the Moor as being somewhat different from the rest of society and some said this was partly to do with inter-breeding and partly due to longevity. The Congleton Chronicle once gave the, perhaps apocryphal, story of the local G.P., Dr Craig, calling on the neighbour of a woman he

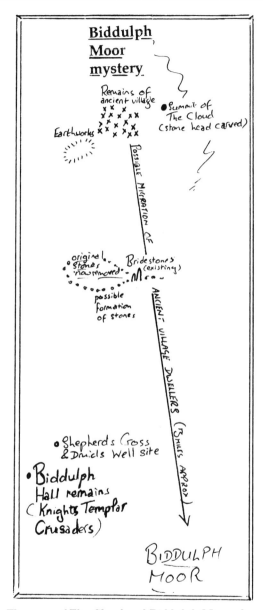

Biddulph Moor mystery

Remains of ancient village
x x x
x x x x x
x x x x x
x x x x x x

● Summit of The Cloud (stone head carved)

Earthworks

POSSIBLE MIGRATION OF

● original stones now removed ●

Bridestones (existing)

possible formation of stones

ANCIENT VILLAGE DWELLERS (3 MILES APPROX)

● Shepherd's Cross & Druids Well site

● Biddulph Hall remains (Knights Templar Crusaders)

BIDDULPH MOOR

The area of The Cloud and Biddulph Moor where the race of people, around whom many legends and traditions have grown, once lived.

had just visited and who was pregnant again at a time when most people elsewhere had long ceased to produce. He asked the neighbour at what age they stopped doing that sort of thing of the Moor and she replied: "It's no good askin meigh, doctor – I'm only 75". The Chronicle's Editor and Proprietor Mr John Condliffe, once told me why he thought the language of the Moor was said to be foreign. It was, he believed, because it was such a broad version of the North Staffordshire dialect – indeed a foreign tongue to the outsider. He told me of a young lad from the Moor telling him many years ago: "Wayn gotten a thray leet arkener." He had, in fact, said his family had recently bought a new radio with three lights, an "arkener" being a "harkener" or listening device, a radio. These people were the salt of the earth, he told me, hard working and often combining a full time collier's job with an equally full time farming activity and proud of their independence. They remind me very much of the good people of The Roaches in North Staffordshire who up until the beginning of the twentieth century were colliers and farmers as well, also immensely proud of their independence.

During the 1930s a considerable amount of research was made into the traditions of Biddle Muir or Moor by Mr Bertram B. Simms, M.B.S.S., M.E.R.S., who held the Diploma of Anthropology at Oxford University. He gave a lecture to the North Staffs Field Club and this was reported fully in the local newspaper, the Congleton Chronicle, at that time. Thanks to the good offices and the friendship of the editor and proprietor of that worthy journal, I was able to find what the anthropologist and other people had to say.

Dealing with the racial origins of the people of Biddulph Moor the Oxford scholar said that since time immemorial traditions have been current in the northern districts of Staffordshire that a number of men from the East settled on the moors around Biddulph or "Bidder" as he thought it was pronounced in local dialect. Sometimes these tales are so given as to render the accounts as though they related to one group of settlers only; in other renderings as though there were several groups each being of a different racial origin; consequently there have been several explanations.

One account says that the folk are descended from seven Saracens brought to England some 900 years ago who settled and married native women of these moors. Another rendering says they were Phoenicians. There is yet another tradition that tells of the settlement of a party of Gypsies who at times are described as "Egyptians". Added to what the researcher termed as the "confusion" but what I would prefer to term the "mystery" is that yet another folk tale has a race of red-haired people resident in the area who were, it is said, the result of the "foreigners" marrying local wives and producing fair haired offspring. He refers to an earlier manuscript written by a Mr Ridgway, a collection of notes taken from early sources and from old Norton folk, that said these "red" people were brought over from the Continent and settled on Norton ridge, not Biddulph Moor, and they were stonemasons. Their common surname was Bailey possibly from the Celtic

106

"baileystyles" denoting those living in new dwellings which later became "newbold" with the same meaning. However, another theory as to this name for local Biddulph Moor people is that the Baileys were in charge of the bailey at the "castle" or manor house on the Moor. To add to the confusion, no very early trace of a Bailey can be found in the Biddulph Parish Registers which commence in 1558 and are some of the earliest in the country. Yet another legend surrounding this family is that they are descendants of a few Scottish rebels who stayed on the Moor after Bonnie Prince Charlie's retreat in 1745.

Two professors in the early twentieth century went as far as to measure the head sizes and the height of a number of local people but their findings showed only what had been said for many years: that the Biddulph folk were in the main smaller than their neighbours and were generally of a darker skin tone and had "full eyes", black pupils that are arresting in their beauty.

One person credited with bringing these dark skinned people to the Moor was the Overlord of Biddulph, Bertram de Verdon, who took part in the third Crusade and died at Joppa in 1192 and was buried at Acre. He, it has been said, brought back some natives of the Middle East and used them as servants at his Hall – then about one thousand meters south west of the last Biddulph Old Hall. However, according to "A History of Leek" by John Sleigh, these servants or whatever, went by the name of "Paynim" and were brought here by another Lord for he wrote: "A Knight Crusader is reputed to have brought over in his train from the Holy Land, Paynim, whom he made bailiff of his estate and from whose marriage with an English woman the present race of "Biddulph Moor Men" are traditionally said to have sprung. Probably this infusion of Saracen blood may account for their nomadic and somewhat bellicose propensities." This Knight Crusader, who is thought to have been a Knight Templar named Ormus de Guidon, was the supposed son of Richard Forestarius, (Richard the Forester) Lord of Darlaston, Buckinhall, Biddulph, etc. Apparently the Biddulph family is directly descended from the royal household of the ancient kingdom of Mercia. According to the Shell Guide to Staffordshire the Biddulph family used these Saracens, who were stonemasons, to produce the intricate carvings at St Chad's Church in Stafford and settled them as bailiffs on the moor. St

Chad is the patron saint of Mercia, the kingdom from which the Biddulph family were connected. The article mentions that these carvings at St Chad's have a "strangely oriental look" and there is an inscription in the Church that reads: "Orme Built me", referring to Ormus de Guidon.

A Knight Templar from an old treatise. Notice the cross he carries and compare with the grave slabs at Biddulph Church.

There is no hard and fast evidence that the crusading knights of Biddulph were Knights Templars although at St Lawrence's Church, Biddulph, there are a number of grave headstones of obvious antiquity and now used as seats around the exterior of the church. On these stone slabs are carvings of crusaders' crosses and several of them are Germanic and very similar to Templar crosses. The nearest known centre for these Knights Templars was at Keele, now a redbrick University, but Hulton Abbey, a Cistercian monastery, owned the pasture rights for sheep on the Moor and at Biddulph and these white-robed monks had strong connections with the Templars. At nearby Leek there was another Cistercian

Abbey known as Dieulacres. But there is far more to these strange crosses on the slabs at Biddulph's ancient Church than meets the eye. A correspondent to the Chronicle newspaper in 1992, Mr Roy Wilding of Chester, thought – like so many other people – that these were Templar crosses. He said the crusader crosses bore typical characteristics of Templar gravestones, of simple design marked with a straight sword and always anonymous. One of the stones has the Greek T or cross with a circle which was a symbol of deity, while another could perhaps symbolise the unity of the Christian and Pagan religions for, he wrote, it has a Crusader cross surmounted on Woden's world ash, denoting the pagan earth cult of Woden and Christianity intertwines.

The grave slabs at Biddulph Church with the Templar crosses.

The Knights Templars were founded in 1188 by Hugh de Payens and this militant order had idealism, religious fervour and chivalry as their inspiration. Originally they dedicated themselves to the defence of pilgrims and the routes to the Holy Land. They took monastic vows and based their rules on the Cistercian Order. As well as the Knights there were lower categories of Templars made up of priests, soldiers and servants. Could these servants have been acquired from the Holy Land, I wonder, and brought over to Biddulph? At the nearby Cistercian Abbey of Hulton, whose ruins are now slap bang in the middle of a housing estate on the fringe of the Potteries, an archaeological dig unearthed the grave of a person who was still wearing a shell badge – the emblem worn by pilgrims to the Holy Land, ensuring them safe passage by the Templars.

But we are getting side-tracked. There is much more to tell about this magical area around Biddulph Moor but for the moment we must look some more at the mysterious race of beings. Were they not descendants of the Saracens at all, but descendants of what are now termed Fairy Folk?

Our search must start just over a mile away from the Moor as the crow flies, on a hill named Bosley Cloud or Cloud End. The steep slopes of this hillside are in the County of Cheshire but a little south west atop the high ridge on more delicate slopes descending to a forest of fine trees we are in Staffordshire, the County boundary being denoted by ancient stone pillars sunk into the ground and carved with a cross. The first clue is given in a letter to the Congleton newspaper early in 1936 and signed by someone calling himself "Magister" with the address of "Kinfare", Hallfields, Biddulph. The correspondent was referring to the mystery of the dark-skinned people of the Moor and wrote: "Of course, one cannot dismiss readily the theory that the Bidder Muir *(sic)* folk were originally Ancient Britons – evidence of the Camp and the site of beehive huts on Cloud End and also of beehive huts at the other end of the millstone grit ridge will bear witness to the occupancy of the higher lands by the Ancient Britons."

There is still evidence of this "Camp" on this high hill and it is thought to be of the late Bronze Age type. It would seem to have been used in far later times than the Bronze Age for up until the nineteenth century when the man-made forest was planted there were hut dwellings in a fine state of preservation. Some historians say these people were known as the Ceangil and a theory is that nearby Congleton is named after them. The Ceangi, it is said, had another camp on Gun Hill just north of Leek, and I have mentioned this area in another book, Myths and Legends of East Cheshire and the Moorlands, as being the place of a very strong earth energy line or ley line. This camp at Gun Hill was close to the "Limes Brittanica" an earthen wall running in a sweeping line through Staffordshire, by Wincle (Cheshire) on by the Goyt Valley pit dwellings and then north of Buxton, an earthwork that linked the mouth of the Severn to the north of the Trent built by the order of the Roman Osterius to keep the Ceangi and the Silures tribe of South Wales from invading territory he had conquered.

Maurice Winnell dowsing at the site of sunken huts on The Cloud.

Another historian called Bertram B. Simms who lived at New-castle in Staffordshire, said the camp was of a type introduced about 1100 BC when the first Celtic tribe, the Goidelic, arrived; that is, 1,000 years before the "Ancient Britons" reached these shores. So even here we have confusion, but undoubtedly the camp is very old in origin and used for a long long time. There is now a conflict of opinion as to whether there was also a hill fort on this intriguing hill. It was described in 1878 as "the remains of a British Hill Fort with its unusual rampart and fosse and was about 790 feet long. The trench was dug out of solid stone and it has been suggested the area was known as the "Cat Stones" which is Celtic meant the place of battle or "site of graves".

An illustration by Maurice Winnell of how the village could have looked. Is this where the strange race of beings came from?

I was first shown the remnants of these huts on the top of the hill by an amateur archaeologist called Maurice Winnell and we had a fine old time investigating them with the aid of divining rods one sunny afternoon. What can now be seen are dugouts with stone sides and entrances over which would be placed roots of wood in the shape of a beehive. More than fifty of these dugouts can still be seen among the heather and the trees and no doubt there are many more. Their entrances all face west and some are considerably bigger than others. Those placed on the higher ground tend to be of the larger variety and the further away from these the smaller they get.

A little way towards the Biddulph Moor stand the enigmatic remains of what was once a huge site of the Ancients known as the Bridestones. This is one of the few long barrows found in Britain with a paved forecourt. The Bridestones or Bridlestsones as they are sometimes known, are investigated in my Myths and Legends book, and I mention they get their name from St Bride which is a Christianised form of a pagan name – Brigit – the fertility goddess of the Brigantes, a tribe more usually associated with the area north of the Mersey or Maeres-sea "boundary river". This area had an immense religious significance to those who have gone before because in a nearby field there is, near to the Cat Stones, an ancient cemetery now in the corner of a field. The lane that goes around this spot is Dial Lane, the name coming from "Deasil" meaning the sunwise direction, the way always taken in ancient ritual ceremony. To go the other way was to go "widdershins" which is against the natural way or anti-clockwise.

How then can we relate to Biddle Moor and the Fairy Folk I have previously hinted at?

Our search now takes us to a book entitled "The God of the Witches" by Margaret Alice Murray, a Fellow of the University College, London, published by Sampson Low, Marston and Co Ltd in 1934. This amazing book mentions the origins of witchcraft and the covens of thirteen people – she likens the Robin Hood and his merry men legends to the witches' covens – and she theorises on the Cult of the Divine King. But, more interestingly in this context, in a chapter called "The Worshippers" she tells of the origins of fairies. She says the real problem today is that we look upon these "fairies" as the tiny elf or the creature with gossamer wings floating on moonbeams and she asks: "Why then were our ancestors so afraid of fairies?"

In tales concerning fairies it is quite common that a person is feared of meeting "The Little People". The most frightening of them all at one time was Robin Goodfellow and only thanks to some of the plays by William Shakespeare did this character become relegated to being a minor character. He was the god of these "little people" and the theory is now generally accepted, she says, that our idea of fairies being tiny is thanks to Shakespeare. In the north of Scotland, in Ireland and in Brittany the fairy is the size of a human being. Dr Murray has obviously done much research and she tells of someone in the sixteenth century consulting the fairies and when doing so always going among "hills" to do so and she reaches the conclusion that fairies were not the tiny Tinkerbells of children's tales but real creatures and, she says, recorded marriages between "mortals" and fairies are proof that they were the same size. She maintains they lived in wild uncultivated parts of the country and though they might sometimes be found in woods they preferred open moors and heaths. And she wrote that their dwellings were built of stone, wattle or turf, and were in beehive form wherein whole families lived together.

A face carved into a rock at The Cloud.

Accounts in legal records and in folklore show, she wrote, a people whose parallel can be found in the Neolithic and Bronze Ages and remains of skeletons in Neolithic burial barrows show that the inhabitants of these islands were short in stature ... and probably had dark complexions. Could this be the reason for the name Brownie? The Neolithic and Bronze age moorland dwellers had circular houses that were sunk into the ground, their floors paved with stone, the lower walls of stone and the upper parts of wattle and daub or turf and the roof, probably turf, was supported by wooden poles. They were built in groups.

So there we are. The fairy folk were just a little smaller than we are today, they were dark skinned and originally lived in beehive huts just like those on the hillside a mile away from Biddulph Moor. In another of my books, "Magic, Myth and Memories", I refer to a book by David MacRitchie written in 1890 and entitled "The Testimony of Tradition". In this he told us that belief in fairies stemmed from the memory of a race of small, dark-skinned people, earthwork dwellers who had "much knowledge of the ancient paths" (ley lines) in their country and were said to have power over the weather and he researched into the theory of the existence of a "conquered race" lurking in moorland and mounds and hanging around farms doing casual work for food but "distrustful of their conquerors' clothing as a badge of servitude". They were thought to be on intimate terms with the local goddess and they would occasionally do odd jobs at farms in return for food. Shirley Toulson in her wonderful book "Derbyshire, Exploring the Ancient Tracks" published by Wildwood House Ltd in 1980 says she feels fairy folk were real. They were pre-Celts, outcasts ... living on the fringe of society and, in all probability she wrote, were used as slaves.

Finally, let us return to the gentleman called Bertram B. Simms who wrote to the local newspaper in 1936 about the Gipsy origins of surnames. One of the many theories about these Moor dwellers, you may recall, was that they were a tribe of Gypsies, and he mentions two names common to the area, Farr and Parr, both derived from the Gipsy names Faa, a derivation of Fay. Faa became Farr and Parr he says. What he did not appreciate was that the name Fay is the original name for Fairy. Fay meant enchanted or bewitched and so Fay-erie was the word used for an enchanted realm and for a state of enchantment. Fays became Fairies and the Greeks used the same word for their "Kindly Ones" called The Furies. Margaret Murray also put forward the theory that fairies would be drawn to wandering bands of Gypsies.

So the clues are there if we wish to take them up. Were the early inhabitants of Biddulph Moor those dark-skinned hut dwellers who walked over from The Cloud just a mile away? As civilisation encroached on that high hill may they possibly have moved to the bleak and desolate moor to keep away from the so-called civilised people?

Healing Powers of the Druid Groves

There are two distinct spots in or around Biddulph Moor that many people say were Sacred Groves of the Celtic Druids in days long gone. One is close by the stone monolith now known as Shepherds' Cross and the other is by an ancient Dolmen at Knypersley Park.

This Dolmen, a Megalithic stone monument, was referred to in Victorian times as a "Druidic Cromlech" and goes by the name of Gawton Stone and is to be found on the Knypersley Hall Estate. This stone monument was used as a burial chamber and has been used also as a Healing Stone. It was formed by three upright stones with a stone on the top. Local legend has long said it was close by a Grove used by the Druids where there was a Well, called Gawton's Well, and this flowed with waters that were used for healing. There is also a natural recess or cave at this spot and according to James Bateman, who was responsible for much of the great landscaping work at Biddulph Grange and formerly lived at Knypersley Hall (and who is thought to have been a student of the mystical), was known as The Hermitage. This is a spot that I would wholeheartedly recommend as being one of the finest, if not the purest, Druid's Grove still surviving in the British Isles.

Please find time to journey to this place, it will be a spiritual upliftment.

Thanks to Staffordshire County Council who have taken over the Knypersley Hall grounds the area is now a Countryside Park and anyone is free to stroll under the lofty trees and to walk by the Serpentine Lake. There is a signposted path that takes the walker to Gawton's Well. This magical and mystical site is surrounded by huge yew trees as old as time. From the hillside, on which there was an ancient burial site, there flows a spring. It falls into a large man-made stone trough and then into the Serpentine Lake. There is an awe-inspiring air around this spot. The huge carved stones now used to form part of a cascade from the spring were undoubtedly part of the ceremonial aspect of the Grove at one time and perhaps it was Bateman and his Landscape Gardener who "tidied" them up and made them look attractive. The water from this spring has long been said to have curative powers. A visit to the Grove itself will cure a great amount of ill-ease.

The Druid's Grove at Knypersley – one of the finest examples of a Grove still in existence.

Gawton's Well at Knypersley. Some of the stones around the well and the channel leading out of it appear to have been upright standing stones at some time.

The dolmen or healing stone at Knypersley from an old drawing by Dr Sainter.
It is known as Gawton's Stone.

There is also an indication of there having been a building in this Grove at one time, perhaps a Hermitage as an adjunct of the curative powers of this natural healing spot. Perhaps the hermit or anchorites came to here not only because of the healing properties but also to make Christian that which was Pagan. Nearby there stood the remains of a standing stone or possibly a stone cross. An interesting spot indeed and it is still possible to use the magic of the place for healing purposes although a lot of people have done their utmost to ensure that the earth magic has been destroyed. A great shame but what these obviously well intentioned people failed to appreciate was that the earth is far more powerful and resilient than we mere humans. Attempts at destruction only really result in suppression. The magic is still there, and the healing powers are still there. Today I would be hesitant to recommend any waters that flow from the ground because of the way we poison the earth with so many chemicals but just to be here and take in the Spirit of the Place is enough.

A short stroll from this Grove there towers the magnificent stone known as Gawton's Stone. It is very similar to a stone dolmen at the land of the high rocks in North Staffordshire, called The Roaches. There there is a boulder known as the Bawd Stone that sits astride smaller boulders and which has been used for healing over the centuries. People would parade to that spot at May Day as recently as the beginning of the twentieth century and then crawl under the boulder so that the Devil would be knocked off their backs. The structure at Knypersley is identical in its function. It is larger than the Bawd Stone and excavation work in the nineteenth century unearthed signs of ancient burials but I do not think this was purely a burial site. Those people were placed there because of the power that comes from these huge rocks. It is quite possible to crawl under the stones in the same way as at the Bawd Stone and the ceremonial creepway is still in evidence. It is still used by people in the hope of being healed.

The second spot thought by some to have been a Druidic Grove is the area around the stone monolith now known as the Shepherds' Cross. This stone monument stands close to the site of Biddulph Old Hall. It is by the side of the road and several stone steps lead up to it. I think it was once an upright stone and it is definitely on a ley line or earth line that lines up with Mow Cop Hill a mile away but at some point masons re-shaped the ancient stone into a Christian cross. This has happened at so many spots where either a Christian cross was carved onto a stone or out of a stone. Across the road there is a wall at the back of which there is all that now remains of the Druids' Grove. Trees, the descendants of the mighty oaks of the past, are now bunched together in this small enclosed spot behind the wall. Out of this grove there was – as at Knypersley – a healing spring that flowed with sweet water. An attempt has been made to capture this water in an ancient stone trough built into the wall.

Possible Druids Grove and well, Biddulph Moor. The Shepherds Cross is across the road.

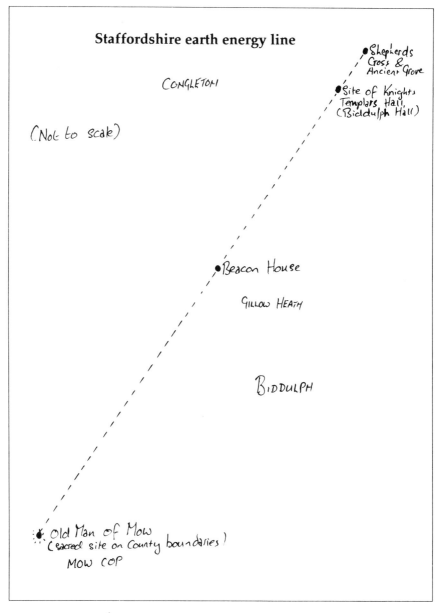

Staffordshire earth energy line

CONGLETON

(Not to scale)

●Shepherds
Cross &
Ancient Grove

●Site of Knights
Templars Hall,
(Biddulph Hall)

●Beacon House

GILLOW HEATH

BIDDULPH

Old Man of Mow
(sacred site on County boundaries)
MOW COP

A ley line from an ancient cross and grove to the Old Man of Mow, a rocky outcrop on top of Mow Cop separating Staffordshire and Cheshire.

There are other places of mystery on and around the Biddulph Moor. Some odd names stand witness to goodness knows what. For instance, we have The Girthing Bank (half way along Congleton Edge from Nick o' th' Hill to Whitemoor Corner), Royal Cottage (perhaps a reference to the troops of Bonny Prince Charlie staying there), Boreham's Hole over Long Edge, David's City, Gibacre Bridge (near Pool Fold), the Beacon House on Congleton Edge, Puddle Bank on the Mossley side of Congleton Edge, and Nettle-beds. Woodhouse Farm near the Grange had a stone with a clearly chiselled biblical passage in use as a front door step and a barn with, most definitely, a very old window inside together with unusual ancient oak beams. In 1664 it was ordered that the remains of Biddulph Castle (or Hall) be preserved "accordynge to Mr Biddulph's own desire towards the repayringe of a little old house of his, not two miles from it." Was Townsend Hall, or Woodhouse Farm, or Biddulph House (at Brown Lees) the house which was repaired with the stone from Biddulph Hall?

Old Nancy of Mixon and the Fairie Folk

In the year 1906 Elijah Cope of Leek put pen to paper and wrote an interesting and enlightening article entitled "Some Local Fairies". I am pleased to say that I have been able to track down his piece in an exceedingly rare book, long out of print.

Elijah wrote that he stayed one night with an old woman named Grindy who lived on a little farm near Mixon in the hills east of Leek. He said that after supper they had a long chat about old times and old people they had both known. "We sat in a room she called the parlour, which was furnished with quaint old oak furniture and some part of the room was wainscoted with oak panelling. As the weather was cold, and partly on account of my visit, a fire had been put in the quaint old grate. We sat till nearly midnight and only a few pieces of wood glowed in the bottom of the grate. I was then startled by what seemed to be several raps on the table and one loud rap on the wainscot near the fire. The old lady did not pay so much regard to the noise as I did but merely remarked that 'Old Nancy has come as usual.' I asked her who Old Nancy was. She replied that she was an old fairy who had been about there goodness knows how long; and that her mother told her about the fairies and counselled her to be good to them and always leave some bits of cake or other food either on the table or other convenient place in the house. Her mother had said that fairies were good and honourable little folk and would never steal anything so long as people were kind to them and that they would do many bits of work in and about the house in payment for food. I asked the old lady if she had ever seen 'Old Nancy' or any of the fairies. 'No', she said, 'I don't know that I have, nor have I any wish to see them. They don't like people to watch them nor to interfere with them in any way.'

Elijah continued that the following morning they had an early breakfast and he walked about the farm buildings and tried to get up a conversation with a servant-man who was busy amongst the cows, but to all his inquiries about fairies, ghosts and witches he gave a vague and evasive reply. Elijah did give the opinion that the noises heard the night before were the sound of oak contracting and expanding because of the heat from the fire.

Towards noon he started on his way home by Mixon Mines and called at a cottage to see a Mrs Frith, whom he cautiously drew into conversation about fairies. She put a shawl or wrap over her head and walked about half a mile on the way home with him in the direction of Mixon Hay Farm. When in the second field from the village she pointed to the lower part of the meadow and told him that her mother had spent hours there watching fairies dance round a ring and had described the different coloured garments they wore. She said she did not think they were so very honest for she had missed many articles of clothing which had been forgotten and left out on the garden fence all night; but added sympathetically: "Poor things, they must have clothes from somewhere and of some kind."

He added that the late Mr Billing who, some years ago (this would be in the nineteenth century) lived on a little farm on the hillside between Morridge End and Hollinsclough was a firm believer in fairies. He was one of the few people he had met with who had seen them dance in a ring, and also seen them about the farm buildings. He learned from him "many strange stories" about fairies and their habit of taking babies from their human mothers and leaving their own children in the place of them. Such children are called changelings or children that have been changed. The following story is typical of many. Most children who were "ill-shapen, dwarves, cripples, or other wise deformed" and especially those who were lacking in speech, were supposed to be changelings. Mr Billing told him that when he was a boy a poor woman who lived at a cottage near him gave birth to a baby that was perfect in every way but very small. When about a month old its mother took it into a hay field and laid it on top of a heap of dried hay. As the sun was very hot she put an umbrella over it. After about an hour or so she returned and found the baby asleep but she fancied its features had changed. The dreadful thought came into her mind that the fairies had taken her baby and left one of their own in its place. Worst of all it did not appear to her, judging from what she had heard about fairies, to be well born or aristocratic, but a common "Hobthurst" which is a fairy of low birth, low habits and by no means industrious, but fond of sitting by the fire and leaning against the hob. She decided, however, to take it home, to be kind to it, and to treat it in every way as her own.

The child grew but little and never learned to talk. Still she was very kind to it hoping that some day or some night fairies might snatch it and return her own – a wish that was never realised. Compensation, however, came in another way. One day, while clearing out an old cupboard that had been built into a recess of the house she found a large number of gold coins wrapped in a piece of old linen rag. She was overjoyed at her good fortune and thankful that she had kept the child and been kind to it; for she was quite satisfied that the fairy to whom the child belonged had put the money there. For over three years she found money occasionally hidden in various parts of the house, chiefly in the thatch. Eventually, however, the child sickened and died from which time, although she diligently searched, she never found a coin of any kind.

Mr Billing was asked if he believed the story to be true. "Of course I do" he replied with some warmth and drawing himself up to his full height. "Certainly. Don't you?"

Elijah Cope continued that most fairy dances that he had heard of had taken place in low boggy ground or damp and undrained meadows. However, the following took place in the Victoria Gardens which were on the lower part of Leek, sloping northwards from the Old Church. A working man rented a piece of garden on the lower part of the ground. After his day's work in the silk mill he went to spend an hour or so weeding some vegetables. When too dark to see the weeds he went to his shed, lit his pipe and sat for some time thinking. Eventually he fell asleep. How long he slept he did not know but it must have been nearly daybreak when he awoke. Going to the door of his shed he was greatly astonished to see a number of little people dancing round a ring, dressed in most gorgeously coloured costumes. Their motion was slow at first but after a little time grew rapid. The man became excited and went a few yards nearer to the dancers to get a better view of them. Still the motion of the dancers became more rapid and in proportion the man became more excited, till finally, losing control over himself, he went close to them and, clapping his hands together in applause, he called out "Well done, my little folks, the one with the blue frock dances best." The spell was broken, the dancing fairies vanished, and the man standing near the spot where the fairies had been rubbed his eyes in utter astonishment.

Elijah had not finished his tales yet, for he said that he remembered when a boy walking with his grandfather from Ipstones to Leek by way of Basford and through the fields where stood the remains of an old stone cross. His grandfather took him a little out of the footpath to a field to show him some rings where fairies were said to dance. The rings were a little larger than an ordinary cartwheel and the ground of a different colour from the other part of the field. Some time later he paid a second visit along with other boys and found the rings were gone. The farmer had given the land a dressing of gas-lime which had killed the fungus that had formed the rings.

Probably the district most inhabited by fairies, he wrote, lies near the bottom lane from Ipstones to Bradnop. There are several farms, mostly of small acreage, called Lady Meadows. The subsoil is clay and the ground wet, except in dry weather. Most fairies of that district seem to have been of a very industrious race. For a piece of cake and a bottle of home-brewed ale they found and restored to their proper places lost iron pins that belonged to the ploughs. They prevented hedgehogs from sucking the milk of cows in the night time. They were encouraged to be about the house by presents of tobacco and little delicacies in the form of food. Their little tobacco pipes were sometimes found in the fields and the ploughman who turned one up whilst ploughing was said to be lucky. The ill-natured housewife who would not encourage nor reward their industry was often in trouble. Her oven would not bake bread properly; her knitting needles fell out; the flat irons were either too hot and burned the clothes or they were too cold and would not iron clothes properly. The things in the house were put in disorder in the night-time. Even her garters refused to remain fastened and her hair would persist in falling down. The worst mischief, however, happened in the night time. The farm dog would bark; crockery was found broken or damaged; the cream was taken from the milk; the wife's Sunday cap was torn to pieces; and the husband's tobacco stolen. In the end it paid the housewife to be kind to the "little folks".

The writer then turned his thoughts towards witches, for he said that some of the witches that he had known had blamed fairies for mischief reputed to them. For instance, when people could not make a light with the flint and steel the mischief was sometimes changed to the fairies and sometimes to the witches and sometimes to both. He mentioned that he had known and been intimately acquainted with witches and had known and seen their methods of work and what are called their black arts "which no respectable and well bred fairy would descend to".

He added that on the whole he had found that fairies are respectable and industrious little folk, very harmless if properly treated and though occasionally given to little acts of roguishness are by no means wholly bad. "They are rapidly dying out" he wrote and continued "Education and science are making their existence intolerable. When they are entirely gone the world will be poorer by the absence of many moral stories told of them, and many high and noble lessons learned from their characters and actions."

There is very little that can be said after that. I have seen a fairy pipe and featured a photograph of it in my book "Magic, Myth and Memories". It was found, still smouldering, in a field in Cheshire so this is not the opportune time to discuss it. However, I would ask you to refer to the thoughts about the Fairy Folk of the Cloud mentioned earlier and how they were supposed to live apart from the human race keeping themselves to themselves. Perhaps these little people were country cousins of those just a few miles down the road, who knows?

When Stoke-on-Trent was a forest

Today, as the visitor to be Potteries surveys the industrialised scene it is almost impossible to envisage how this area used to be and what it contained before the iron, pottery and coal industries took over. There are still clues to be found if we should search for them, although, in the main, the people who now inhabit the Potteries are descendants of the industry; their forefathers came into the area from the outside in search of work in the thriving industrial sector. When the five towns were tiny hamlets there were only a few people about although there are names such as Sneyd, Colclough and Bagnall that tell the inquirer those people had forebears who lived within this area before industry took over.

The folk themselves are a friendly lot; they are proud of their area and they have a language all their own. A "Pot Herb" is proud to be known as such and is proud to talk the North Staffordshire language. This is as near to Old English as you can get these days; it is a direct descendant of the language talked in Chaucerean times. It is a bit of England as it used to be.

Within this land there is a Druid's Grove already discovered at Knypersley and there is a remnant of the old religion at the nearby Gawton Stone, a huge boulder with a creepway used for healing. And there is much more to be found. Goldenhill denotes the Shining One, the god of the ancients who lived on top of a hill; there is Shining Tor to the North that has the same derivation. A 'shining' or 'golden' hill was a place where people not of this world, the fairy folk or the spirits of the ancients, would meet and these were the places that superstitious countryfolk would not venture to if possible. At Stoke itself, meaning a fortified stockade, and the collective name so often (wrongly) given to this area there is the Church of St Peter and nearby is the base and trunk of an ancient preaching cross. Was this cross, I wonder, a stone monolith before it was used for preaching. Perhaps in earlier times it was used for praying to, not preaching from. Stoke was most probably a fortified place holding out from the old Britons who took refuge in the high Staffordshire moorlands.

Before the Normans came here the whole area was forest; it was part of the ancient Forest of Lyme. Newcastle under Lyme still bears witness to this and Burslem, or Burs Lyme, also stands testimony to the old wooded land. The area was not only densely forested but it was hilly as well and thus it would have been very sparsely inhabited. Those who ventured into the trees of ash, elder, oak and hazel were the ones who went to the Groves therein, the Druids and Ovates, the initiated ones ... the Celtic keepers of the old religion.

Goldenhill – once a sacred site to the Shining Ones.

Hanley, now the shopping centre of the district, derives its name from Hean Lea, a high meadow; probably a clearing on high ground above the forest. Have you noticed how it always seems to be windy at Hanley? It's a phenomenon that can be put down to its geography, I feel.

And as for Tunstall, this is probably of Angle origin and belonged in later Norman times to the Earls of Chester. Longton was a tiny hamlet; in 1773 there were only 180 families scattered over what was then known as the Common and this area was called Lane End until the middle of the nineteenth century. Another of Arnold Bennett's Five Towns is Fenton; this was one of the few places within the whole of Staffordshire where an Englishman, Alward, was allowed to keep his land after the Normans came to these shores.

The area has sired many great men and, although not a true man of the Potteries, canal builder and engineer James Brindley has been claimed as one of Stoke-on-Trent's own. He was born in Derbyshire and came to Leek at an early age, but he did much work for that Master Potter Josiah Wedgwood and one of his main works in this area was the Harecastle Tunnel. Of this it is said that it was placed in such a direction that the sun rising on his birth date shone right through it. I do not know if this is correct, but it might be a worthy exercise for someone at some time or other.

There are remnants of magic and mystery remaining within certain place names in this area; Cross Heath implies there having been a stone monolith, perhaps Christianised, being there. Stanfield implies a stone in a clearing.

And then, of course, there is the area of Abbey Hulton that once was home to Hulton Abbey. This Cistercian monastery was destroyed by Henry VIII but, despite the years and despite it being in the middle of a large housing estate, there is much evidence of it still there. One of the intriguing finds recently has been the skeleton of a deformed woman, her spine curved and this person would only have been some four feet tall. She was pregnant. Her remains had been buried within the confines of the Monastery itself... what, I wonder, was the story behind this poor person? And then there is the discovery of a pilgrim's body. This person's remains were discovered during an archaeological dig and he was still wearing the leather boots he must have trudged the pilgrims' way with. He was wearing a shell, the symbol of a pilgrim, and he would have been given warmth and shelter, plus food and drink, at the Abbey. Where was he going to, I wonder?

Cult of the Head

Perched high on the Staffordshire moorlands and snuggling right up to the Cheshire border is a stately home, now tastefully divided into "executive" homes. It is set amid some of the finest parkland there can be found anywhere in the entire county and beyond. It is a very private place; visitors are only welcome by appointment and it has been such not just for the few years that is has been made into a number of homes but for the centuries upon centuries that people have lived there.

Swythamley Hall started life, no doubt, as a hunting lodge within the densely forested woodland that abounded in that area. It was the Forest of Lyme, the dividing forest that separated the Palatine of Cheshire from the rest of the world and it was also, in its time, a grange for the Cistercian Abbey of Dieulacres a few miles to the south.

This Hall, or Manor House or, as some have described it, a Castle at one time, has been all things to all people over hundreds of years. And it has been a very special place to many. The land on which it has been built has been a Neolithic burial ground, a Royal burial ground for a Norman prince; it has been visited by royalty and it has been the setting for a medieval saga involving a Celtic cult and Arthurian legend. And it has been much more; it has been the centre of a ghostly haunting and it has been the home to larger than life characters who knew of the Old Ways as well as the new.

I make no excuse for mentioning Swythamley Hall once more. I have alluded to its mysteries in two of my previous works and every time I think I have finished writing about this place I am drawn back to it once more, like a magnet attracting iron filings.

This ancient place still has strong earth energy lines going through it and it is an area full of psychic energy. A Neolithic burial ground is now known as Knight's Lowe in the grounds of the Hall. At one time there was a stone column or cross standing on it, exactly the same as the one nearby at Cleulow Cross, just across the Cheshire border. At one period in its history it was removed and replaced a few metres or so away and, perhaps at the same time, it was found necessary to place a stone cross on its top.

Knight's Lowe could have some bearing on the fact that the saga of Gawain and the Green Knight was set in this spot. This was where Gawaina relaxed at "Bercilak's Castle" before fighting the foliate-headed Green Knight at the Green Chapel (nearby Lud Church).

The Hall itself has had a chequered history, being rebuilt a few hundred years ago and part of the rebuilt hall being ravaged by fire. It was the site of the royal hunting lodge for the Norman Kings within the forest and it was utilised by the Cistercian monks for a grange and a lodge within the forest. Later, it was purchased from the De Trafford family by the Brocklehurst family – a remarkable dynasty who rose to power and glory with the rise of the local silk industry and then almost completely died out in the mid-1900s. Eventually, the last of the male line with the name Brocklehurst, Sir Philip, died in the early '70s and the estate was sold off in bundles, the antiques and curios within the Hall were auctioned and the Hall itself was purchased for transcendental meditation purposes. If this all sounds familiar to you then I apologise, for I have gone over this before and must get on to new discoveries.

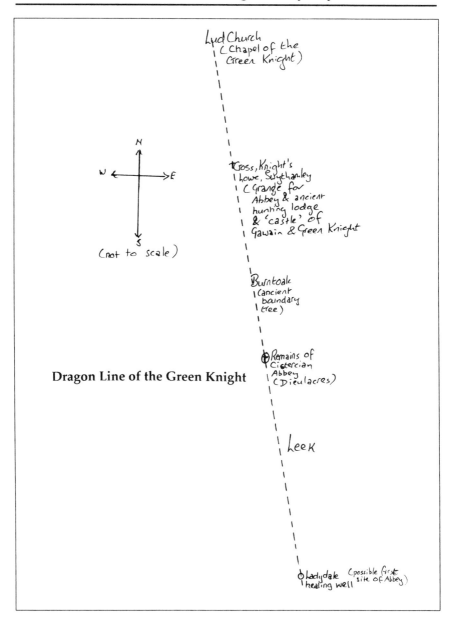

Lud Church
(Chapel of the
Green Knight)

N

W ⟵ ⟶ E

S

(not to scale)

Cross, Knight's
howe, Swythanley
(Grange for
Abbey & ancient
hunting lodge
& 'castle' of
Gawain & Green Knight

Burntoak
(ancient
boundary
tree)

Dragon Line of the Green Knight

Remains of
Cistercian
Abbey
(Dieulacres)

Leek

Ladydale (possible first
healing well   site of Abbey)

A ley line connecting ancient sites, many associated with the legend of Gawain
and the Green Knight.

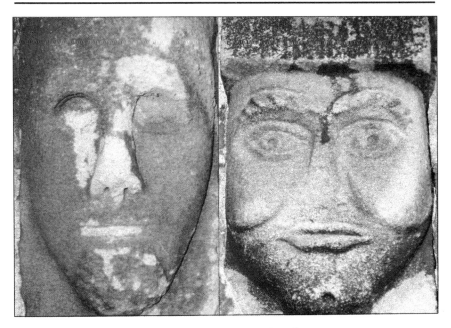

Two stone heads at Swythamley.

I had the pleasure of being invited to the Hall by the present owner, Mr Richard Naylor, and was allowed to view Knight's Lowe and the cross and whilst doing so could not help to be impressed by the number of stone carvings of heads there are about the Estate. Mr Naylor did not know their origins but thought they may, possibly, be Victorian. I took photographs of them (some having been included in a charming dovecote) and have studied them and have asked others to do likewise. The consensus of opinion is that some could be as young as Victorian, others could be medieval, and may possibly have come from the Monastery of Dieulacres; but some are most certainly far older. Undoubtedly someone or other has collected stone heads over the years. The older ones are probably Celtic and are connected with the Celtic Cult of the Head. Perhaps it is too much of a coincidence that this beheading cult that is shown to its full glory in the saga of Gawain and the Green Knight should, if you will pardon the pun, rear its head with the Celtic stone figures now to be found at the spot that is most probably the setting for part of the saga, Oh, and it is also quite probably that this lengthy talk written in North Midlands dialect was penned by a Cistercian monk obviously familiar with the area and familiar with Celtic customs and traditions. Would it be stretching the imagination too far to wonder whether this monk could possibly have been at Dieulacres Abbey just down the road?

This strange carved stone head was discovered many years ago at Bagnall in North Staffordshire by a farmer. It is now in the back garden of a gentleman in Leek (photo Mike Oldham).

Was there a Celtic influence many hundreds of years ago at Swythamley? Some clues may still be there, although the years have changed both the hall and the grounds. The Celts, as with other people of the past, were strongly attuned to the Earth. Neolithic man found the spot mystical for he buried his leaders or chiefs at the spot now known as Knight's Lowe. The Saxons thought it special because they erected a stone cross there (or, to be more precise, an upright stone carved in the form of a phallus) and the Normans thought it special because an Earl of Chester was responsible for bringing the monks to the area had his heart buried there, according to tradition, after he had died at the Hunting Lodge or whatever was on the site of the Hall in those far off days. And, even in the twentieth century a religious order founded on the faraway sub Continent of India thought it of such spiritual value that they set up a Centre for meditation and upliftment there.

So why not the Celts? If some of these stone heads are Celtic in origin then our search is over. The Cistercian holy man who wrote the Sir Gawain and the Green Knight poem was versed in Celtic tradition, surely rather an odd thing for a White Monk in or about the 1400s ... unless that monk was a Celt himself, coming over to these shores from Ireland, one of the last bastions of the Celtic race. Might he not have seen and recognised connections with the Celts at Swythamley in those far-off days? It is a theory and theory it must remain for now.

A delightful and rare photograph of Sir Philip Brocklehurst, the last of the dynasty at Swythamley Hall. He is with his pet badger; the family's name is derived from "the place of the badger". He knew much of the legends of the area and was probably responsible for collecting the many stone heads at the Hall (courtesy Joyce Matthews).

Another rare and delightful picture. This is of two llamas that escaped from the private zoo of Courtney Brocklehurst during the second world war along with wallabies and other species. These two are pictured just next to Lud Church, the Green Chapel, in Back Forest.

However, before we conclude this quest, perhaps I could mention another channel of investigation ... psychic help. A visit to the area with my wife, who I had not told of the search for the Green Man and the Celts, was to prove interesting. She sensed, or saw, white-robed figures within a thickly wooded forest. Now these could have been the white-robed monks who used the area as a grange for tending sheep and other animals or it could have been the white-robed Druids of the Celtic peoples. But these white-robed people were tending a sick person (again it could have been the monks or the Druids) and they were giving that sick person, who way lying on the ground, a drink of something or other. Then they began to chant as if in prayer. They held their hands above their heads and were speaking in a strange language ... and that was it. Nothing else.

But that was enough. The language could have been Latin or it could have been the language of the Middle English Celts; it is impossible to say. But had those white-robed people have been Christians they would, probably, have prayed in the traditional manner with hands together and there would have been the symbol of the crucifix present. But there did not seem to be. There was nothing else to point towards them being Celtic either, except that it felt right. Now there is no way that any learned historian or any sceptical person would possibly accept that as any sort of proof of anything and I appreciate that. All I can say is what was seen.

8

The Heartlands

Ghosts of Robin and Marian

It was on the Boxing Day of 1993 that I and Hilary travelled into the Staffordshire Heartlands to pay a visit to the Morris Men. Full of Christmas pud we may have been but the day was full of magic. The air was crisp and the sun was low in the crystal blue sky. The roads were treacherous, many ungritted (I would think because of the holidays and lack of traffic) and an intended diversion to Hollington saw our car sliding on a sheet of ice that had once been a road. Torville and Dean would have been proud of us and, more thanks to front wheel drive and our spirit guardians than my driving skills, we got to grips with the situation.

Our journey ended in the Market Square at Uttoxeter where a crowd was enthralled with the antics of three groups of Morris men, and one of their number, Jack Brown. Here at Uttoxeter on that crisp Yuletide noontime I watched them cavort their ancient rituals and mulled over the fact that history and tradition had come full circle. The Morris Men have ancestral connections with the legends of Robin Hood and the Green Man, the Horned God and the fertility spirits of the wild wood. Uttoxeter has understated connections with the legends of the Man in Green and his Lady and just down the road at Abbotts Bromley the mystical and magical Horn Dance, with Robin and Marian and memories of Herne the Hunter, is still re-enacted after an unbroken span of countless hundreds, indeed thousands, of years. Prominent among those Morris Men who were entertaining in the Uttoxeter Market Square on that day was a happy and sociable person called Jack

Brown, who has had the honour of being one of the very few "outsiders" to have been invited to participate in the pagan Horn Dance just down the road.

Morris Men in Uttoxeter Market Place on Boxing Day, 1993.

The area around Uttoxeter, Loxley and Abbotts Bromley was heavily wooded before and after the Norman Conquest and almost the entire County of Staffordshire could have been divided geographically into a number of "forests" or "chases". The land around Uttoxeter (or Utchetter as it is known locally) abutted onto other woodland and wild land that stretched over to Nottingham and the greenwoods of Sherwood in the east, the Chase of Cannock to the south and joined with the New Forest and the Forest of Lyme in the north (the word Lyme denoting a boundary and in this instance it being the boundary of the Palatine of Cheshire). It is said that a squirrel, a red one of course, could have hopped from tree to tree from the Irish Sea to the North Sea in those times without touching the ground. This woodland, densely populated with mighty oaks and hardy ash, was a place where men ventured only if they were forced to. Foresters carried on their trade, poachers did likewise, and the gentry hunted happily. It was also a place where the Spirit of the Wood lurked. This Spirit took on other names and disguises as well ... the Green Man, Jack-in-the-Green, the King of May and Robin of the Wood, all of whom later became Robin of the Hood.

Robin Hood and Maid Marion

Today many assume that Robin Hood along with his Merry Men and his girlfriend Marian were historic personages who hid in the Forest of Sherwood, harassed the Sheriff of Nottingham and King John, robbed the rich to help the poor, and wore rather fetching outfits of green but whether or not any of the characters, apart from King John and the Sheriff, were real-life people is highly debatable. I personally would go so far as to say Robin Hood definitely did not exist as a person but he and his entourage were very much alive as earth and wood spirits in the minds and memories of our ancestors. Nottingham has laid claim to these characters and a thriving tourist industry is centred around their myths and legends but this is a claim that can be proved unjust. Yes, the Spirit of the Green Man haunted Sherwood Forest but it haunted the Forests of the Staffordshire heartland as well. It haunted the souls of the people of Staffordshire just as much as those of the good folk of Nottingham; but Staffordshire people kept their knowledge to themselves.

In traditional legends, Robin Hood was known as Robin of

Loxley, or Locksley, before his lands were "unjustly" taken from him by the wicked Normans. The 1865 book "History of the Town of Uttoxeter" by Francis Redfern says of the village close by Uttoxeter: "Loxley has attained a degree of celebrity as being, if not the birth-place of Robin Hood, at least the scene of many of his bold exploits. An old chronicle of the date of 1621 relates that after his return to Loxley from his visit to his Uncle Gamwell in Warwickshire, after certain inquiries concerning his men 'Clorinda came by, the queen of the shepherds was she', with whom he fell in love. 'Sir Roger, the parson of Dubridge, was sent for in haste; He brought his mass book, and bid them take hands, And joined them in marriage full fast.'

"According to the tradition of the neighbourhood the honeymoon was spent in the beautiful demesne of Loxley; and many engaging stories have been related by the gardener of Loxley ninety years ago – respecting both the rendezvous and doings of this celebrated outlaw. These lines are supposed to have reference to the gallant freebooter on his return to Loxley, after the marriage with his wife: 'Bold Robin Hood and his sweet bride, Went hand in hand into the green bower; The birds sung with pleasure in those merry green groves' O this was a most joyful hour.'"

Robin Hood's hunting horn at Loxley Hall, from a nineteenth century drawing.

The book mentions that at Loxley there was Robin Hood's Horn, formerly in the ownership of the de Ferrers family at Chartley. This family's name comes from them having been blacksmiths or farriers for the invading Norman army and they were granted lands by William the Conqueror as reward. Their coat of arms, three horseshoes, is still kept alive in a number of public house names. This horn then probably came into the possession of the family of Kynnersley by the marriage of Johanna, daughter of Thomas de Ferrers, to John de Kynnardesleye. It bears the initials "R.H." and the three horseshoes.

But Robin's affinity with the Staffordshire heartland does not end there. I came across an enchanting book entitled "Midland Leaves" by W. Byford Jones who wrote articles for the Express and Star, Wolverhampton, under the nom de plume of Quaestor in those balmy days before the Second World War. The book was published in 1934 and contained re-prints of articles he had written for the paper. On page 156 he finds himself strolling in the Royal Forest of Needwood and had walked half way across a narrow lane that links Hoar Cross with Barton. He described it as a lovely lane that rose and fell with the mechanical regularity of a switchback and its banks were smothered by bluebells. At New-church he turned up Six Lane Ends and entered the forest where he met some foresters and struck up conversation. "Over Yonder" said one forester "is a stone which marks the spot where Robin Hood lay hidden in a thicket to escape from the King's men."

The author replied that he did not know that Robin Hood was in any way associated with Staffordshire. He was answered: "Robin Hood and his archers stole deer from this forest and practised highway robbery nor far off. They used to come down here when Sherwood Forest was too hot for their liking. Have you not heard the ballad about Robin Hood being married on Stafford-shire soil up at Tutbury Fair to a wench named Clorinda? The parson from Doveridge tied the knot."

He went on to relate that he also learned that on the fringe of the forest, not far from Six Lane Ends, there was a house which, legend had it, was built on the foundations of the one in which Robin Hood was born. This tradition is oral history that cannot be authenticated, he wrote.

The story of Robin marrying Clorinda, or Clorina in some documents, was from "A new Ballad of Bold Robin Hood, Shewing His Birth, Breeding, Valour and Marriage at Titbury Bull Run-ning." The "bull running" took place at Tutbury Castle during the 14th century.

In this lengthy ballad, Robin asks the lady to marry him and she says she cannot because she must be at "Titbury Feast" and adds: "If Robin Hood will go hither with me, I'll make him the most welcome guest". Robin agrees and they, accompanied by Little John, journey to Tutbury carrying a freshly killed deer as an offering for the feast. During their journey they fight with eight ruffians in a forest but after successfully vanquishing them they go to the feast and are married.

In a Celtic tale the hero, called Owein, passes through an enchanted forest and is waylaid by the keeper of the forest who has power over all the animals and he kills a stag to impress the hero. Likewise, the horned god, Cernunnos, is depicted as having power over animals and has been referred to as "the Bull Horned". The connections between this tale in a forest, the hero being waylaid, the killing of a stag and the journey to the bull should not be ignored. Especially when we shall look at the Horned Dancers of nearby Abbotts Bromley in a short while – complete with the archer Robin Hood and Maid Marian.

Tutbury Castle, where Robin Hood and his bride walked to after being married at Doveridge. Here they witnessed the old and cruel ceremony involving minstrels chasing a maddened bull.

The spectacular doorway to Tutbury Church. A strong energy line connects this building with the castle site.

Tutbury Castle belonged at the time of this ballad to John of Gaunt, the fourth son of Edward III who became Duke of Lancaster. This brother of the Black Prince owned not only Newcastle and Tutbury Castles but also nearly 300 other manors in various parts of England. In 1361 he was granted the estates that had belonged to Thomas, Earl of Lancaster, and then after forty years Tutbury Castle was rebuilt. He had married Constance of Castile, a Spanish princess. At Tutbury Castle Gaunt and his wife lived in almost regal splendour spending long days in hunting in Needwood Forest and evenings in feasting the high nobles who thronged to the castle. He instituted a Court of Minstrels which had officers, awarded certificates to players and heard complaints against them. In August each year the Court of Minstrels assembled and went to church. A special sermon was preached after which the "King" of the minstrels held a "Court". Bull running followed, a maimed bull being provided by the Abbot and chased by the minstrels. They got the bull angry by cutting off its horns, ears and tail, covering it with soap and blowing pepper up its nose. It was then let loose and the winner of the "contest" who received the boast as the prize was the one who was first to cut away part of its hair while it was still in Staffordshire.

Edward III, the father of the owner of Tutbury Castle, founded the Order of the Garter, thought by some to be a secret society akin to the covens of witches. Whether this was so is debatable, but Lichfield is undoubtedly the place where the Order was first formulated. When Edward returned from is victories at Crecy and Calais, Lichfield was chosen for one of those splendid scenes of chivalry by which the English King and his nobility celebrated the success. There were water sports on Minster Pool and a tournament in which the King and seventeen of his knights jousted against the Earl of Lancaster and thirteen others. Ladies and gentlemen alike wore blue cloaks and white hoods and the ladies wore masks or visors, nearly 300 being provided. It is thought the Order of the Garter may have been suggested by some incident at these games and was certainly in the same year as the tournament. There were at first twenty five knights of the Garter, more than half of whom had fought under the Black Prince in France.

They included Audley and Wrottesley, both members of great Staffordshire families; the Earl of Lancaster and Lord Stafford were other Staffordshire nobles among the original twenty five. And some of the revenues of Uttoxeter Rectory were afterwards made over to the Chapel of the Garter at St George's, Windsor Castle. Gaunt was friend and protector of John Wycliffe whose followers were known as Lollards. There is an, oft-repeated, story concerning the Lollards and Lud Church, a chasm in the northernmost part of Staffordshire, and there is another tale of Little John being buried at that self-same spot. I have mentioned this mystical and magical place that towers above the River Dane in two of my previous books. It is the supposed Green Chapel of the North Midlands saga of Gawain and the Green Knight and it is the spot where Bonny Prince Charlie is said to have stopped to rest on his march southwards to claim the Throne of England. The story concerning the Lollards is that they held secret services in this remote spot and the granddaughter of one of their leaders was murdered therein. This Chapel in the Forest is dedicated to the Celtic god Llud and is well worth a visit, if only to take advantage of the Earth Magic that is still retained.

The Horned God

Each year, in early September, men of the village of Abbotts Bromley between Uttoxeter and Lichfield act out a ritual as their predecessors have done for countless centuries. Their Horn Dance is rooted in time, set in tradition, and has its foundations deep in the magical earth. Today this pagan fertility dance has the full backing of the church having encouraged the dancers to change the timing of their annual festivities from the midwinter solstice ritual to the Monday following the first Sunday after the 4th of September! It used to be performed on New Year's Day and at Twelfth Night but there came a time when the dancers had to join the Christian Church or banish the ritual. Compromise won and a harmless date, coinciding with the Wakes Holidays of the nearby industrial towns so the day trippers could come to spend their cash, was decided upon.

The Church did what it had done throughout the centuries and took an "if you can't beat 'em, join 'em" attitude, but it is still wary of the pagan symbolism of this ritual, bringing in the Horned God, fertility, the Lords of the Wild Wood and much more. Church authorities have now agreed to allow the antlers, worn by the dancers, to be stored in the church, but for many centuries they were not let near the place. And when the dancers perform their ritual for the vicar on the Horn Dance Day, two characters are omitted – the Fool (who used to be a lewd character) and Maid Marian (a man dressed as a woman, the She Male, who denotes fertility). Marian is not dressed in a sexual sense, rather "She" is a comic character and, indeed, was the for-runner of the panto-mime dame of today. She represents the male and female coupling and connects with the Maid Marian legends joining with the Green Man, Robin Goodfellow, Robin of the Hood, Puck, the Lord of the Wildwood and Herne the Hunter ... the Horned God depicted by the Abbotts Bromley Horn Dancers.

So what of these Horn Dancers? I was fortunate enough to hear of their all-day ritual from a chap who is now the King of the Staffordshire Morris Men, Jack Brown, who I have mentioned as being at Uttoxeter when I and my wife visited on Boxing Day. Jack is a member of the English Folk Song and Dance Society and is an authority on the Dancers. So much so that, although he is not from

146

Abbotts Bromley, he had joined the Dancers on many occasions and has had the honour of leading them on their perambulations in and around the village.

I have witnessed the ritual and found it fascinating, but Jack has been able to tell me the ins and outs of this (now) unique event. He has been in the thick of the all-day ritual and knows what it is really all about.

There are three white reindeer horns used, the heaviest being about 25lbs and the lightest about 13lbs. There are also three blue horns (as they are known) but nowadays they are painted brown for some reason not appreciated by many. They were, quite possibly, black at one time as the dance involves the ritual ceremony of revival and black would have stood for death with the white, of course, being life. Jack said the dance was at least 1,000 years old but I would put it a thousand or so years back beyond that. The main character is the horse, the hobby horse, and there is the boy with a bow and arrow (Robin?) a man-woman or she-male sometimes known as Maid Marian relating to fertility. This character carries a wooden ladle with a hole in it and a stick ... a phallic connotation. Then there is Fool who carries a bull's bladder and hits people with it if they get in the way of the procession. He also hits the dancers if they flag. Then there are the musicians: a triangle player who is a young boy (and whose grandfather has usually taught him how to play the instrument the morning of the dance) and the accordionist. This accordionist would probably have been a fiddle player in medieval times and a drummer before then. The music nowadays can be anything, usually jigs or reels, but a leading Folk Song authority, Cecil Sharpe, noted in 1910 that there was one tune and he recorded it for posterity in the third volume of "Dances of Northern England". It is generally called "The Old Tune" and Jack remembers one Abbotts Bromley character by the name of Jim Powell who danced the Horn until he was 74 and always wanted this tune, indeed not being willing to dance to anything else. It was the pure tune, he said.

He describes the dance thus: the leader breaks off and spars with the others. At a given order the two lines face; the hobby horse facing the Bow and Arrow (Robin) and the Fool facing the Man-Woman. The leader calls all the instructions in a curious way. "Oh" means "Off" and "Ay" means "Face". "Oo" means "Through". It looks like a fight between deer and they clash during the dance.

Maid Marian at Abbotts Bromley Horn Dance at the beginning of September each year. This character, a man dressed as a woman, is a traditional she-male or man/woman figure that is used in ceremonies throughout the country. The Antrobus Soulers in Cheshire have a similar figure; probably denoting fertility. The Maid Marian name could have associations with local legends of the Man in Green and Marian. Some say "The Merry Men" title is a corruption of "Marian's Men". Marian, in turn, could be a form of "Mary" the Virgin ... earlier the Earth Mother.

The Fool at the Horn Dance, Abbotts Bromley.

The procession starts at the church. The warden has lined up the horns (that are hanging on the walls of the church for the rest of the year) and the characters arrive at eight a.m., dressed in their costumes. They then line up in their processional order and perform the first dance of the day for the vicar but the Man-Woman and the Fool do not dance for the man of the cloth. These are the two fertility symbols and it has obviously been deemed unwise for them to perform. They collect money from the vicar and then proceed to the Butter Cross. After dancing there they walk down the road and up Goose Lane and dance, nowadays, around some new houses. Two characters knock on doors and then walk through the lanes to a farm where they again dance and where they used to be given parsnip wine. Another farm is then visited. It used to be Cotterills but now belongs to Halls and the procession lines up and during the dance the farmer and his son are invited to dance for three or four minutes. This is so they can benefit from the fertil-

149

ity and good fortune ritual. When it was Cotterills there were mugs of tea especially "stewed" for about a week before. Now it's tea, coffee, sandwiches and cakes.

The Horn Dancers do not practice. Newcomers learn as they go along.

After this farm they go around the reservoir and to the village of Admaston. There they dance on a lawn and are given a cup of tea and sandwiches. Down the lane they go to the Post Office, knocking on the doors on their way and bringing "luck and fertility" to the occupants as they do so (and also collecting money in return) then on to Blithfield Hall, the home of the Bagot family, where they congregate outside for noon. After they have danced at mid-day the dancers are introduced to Lady Bagot by their appointed leader. They dance four or five times in the space of an hour before lunch is taken at the Hall. Then it is back to Abbotts Bromley and from about three o'clock they are centred on the village. They visit the landlords at the pubs (and invite them to join in the dance to bring luck, prosperity and fertility) and in days now gone they used to have salads and bread and butter and tea at tea-time but today it is fish and chips at The Crown.

After the feast it is out of the Crown, up School Lane, turn left and then into The Crescent. After a little rest it's through the grounds of Abbotts Bromley Girls' School coming out at the top of the village on the Rugeley side and back to the Coach and Horses where there are more sandwiches and a drink (or two). When the processional dance is concluded the Dancers line up and march back to the church where there is, nowadays, a short service usually attended by visitors who have witnessed the ceremony.

Jack told me that, traditionally, the horse is killed for the good of the community of Abbotts Bromley. The boy with the bow and arrow shoots and hits the head (it had to be regularly painted because of this). In the olden days the horse was brought back to life after a while but now it is revived almost immediately. The horns used to be kept in the old village hall and then they were kept in the Goat public house and then in the Belfry of the church but now in the church itself, hanging on the wall.

Foliate head carvings at St Mary's Church, Stafford. These head figures could represent re-birth (as does the dance at Abbotts Bromley).

151

Field of the Dead? Centre of the World?

It is no wonder that the Christian Church chose Lichfield as its spiritual and cultural centre for this part of the world. For many centuries the Diocese of Lichfield controlled a great proportion of the country's Churches. It has long been a special place and it is, to this day, special.

There are some who say that Lichfield is the very spiritual centre of the world or, at least, the centre of England: a sweeping statement indeed and one that requires further attention. The omphalos or navel (belly button to you and me) of the world is here, so it is said by some. Many believe that the world, like the human body, is made up of a head, body, heart, etc, and, like the body, there are several "shakra" points like the top of the head, the forehead (where the "third eye" is said to be); the throat, the chest, the diaphragm, the navel, the groin and the base of the spine. I know that in mentioning these spots I am opening the floodgates for people to tell me I am wrong, because different beliefs, either religious or spiritual, have variations on this theme but I am more or less treading the middle path. I think, with these examples.

So, just like the body, the Earth has these spots, we are told. And some are of the absolute belief that Lichfield is the navel of the Earth. The centre from which the newborn are attached, the life-giving source. It is fair to say that there are many other claimants to this: Oxford, Kingston and Glastonbury to name but a few. I would recommend the works of Bob Trubshaw, "Mercian Mysteries" editor for the full spectrum of this vast subject. But if it is the centre of life, why has it been given the name that means field of the dead? Perhaps, it is argued, because that name was given far later than when it was first realised it was a special point upon the earth. (It may also be 'clearing in the grey wood'.)

It was probably between the second and the fourth century that this special place got its present name. The area has, for countless centuries, been, if nothing else, the centre of pilgrimage not just for Christians but for the worshippers of the earth, sun and moon before them. People have flocked to this area because of the spiritual and mystical associations it has.

According to some reports, it was during the end of the Roman occupation of this country that the Field of the Dead earned its name. During the fourth century after Christ the Romans, who had by that time become Christian themselves, set about slaying

Christians on these shores. But why? The Romans had, it would seem, half-heartedly become Christian and had given lip-service to the religion but still reverting to their Old Ways. The Roman occupiers did not, as a rule, tell those they were occupying how to conduct their religion and the Christian doctrine taught, in the main, its followers to obey the earthly rulers. All well and good, it would appear, but the Romans did from time to time set about what became known as the Slaughter of the Innocents and Christians were put to the sword. Perhaps the Christian faith was becoming stronger than the might of Rome, who knows. The very first British martyr was Alban who was put to death by the Romans and he is now remembered in the name of the town of St Albans.

It could very well have been at this point in our history that the Christians who had flocked to the holy and spiritual town of Lichfield were put to death. The coat of arms of Lichfield has, today, three martyrs with crowns and it is thought this could refer to this massacre.

The story goes that Amphibalus who was a disciple of the English holy man and martyr to be canonised as St Alban fled after his leader was slain. From just outside St Albans, at a place known as Verulam, he fled along one of the few thoroughfares in the country – the road known as Watling Street and said to be a Roman Road, but in point of fact it had been a road long before the Romans came to our shores. This road connected the holy place of Verulam with the holy place of Lichfield and the disciple of St Alban and his followers hid in the forests just outside the Staffordshire town.

People flocked to this holy man who was at the mystical place. As each day went by, more and more came to him and many of them stayed. These people included rich Romans from the Roman garrison of Letocetum but the majority were Middle Englanders. It has been recorded that a few came from as far afield as Northumberland and if this is correct it emphasises not only what a "draw" this man was but also what an attraction the area was.

More than likely, these Christians were on their own, for all around them were worshippers of other religions; probably more followers of the Earth Cults than were followers of the Christ Cult. The story goes that a group of Roman soldiers found them; whether by chance or not is not made clear and they slew the Christians in their hundreds ... and some say in their thousands. Their bodies were left where they lay and the wolves of the forest had a feast.

Lichfield Cathedral: the site of an extremely ancient centre of worship, but perhaps St Chad's nearby is an older centre. It is also said to be the scene of a haunting.

The local legend said that for centuries after, those forests were haunted by the souls of the early Christians.

Another version has Welsh raiders coming east via Watling Street who were the murderers. As the Church grew stronger and the Royal Household of Mercia became Christian, then Lichfield was given over to the followers of Christ; but up until the sixth century it was a holy place for followers of other religions as well as the Christians, who made the place a missionary settlement; however the Christian Church was, by then, the strongest religion.

Such was the holiness of the area that one of the most important Christian people in the entire British Isles decided that this was the spot for him. He was St Chad, the Holy Man. Chad was at one time Abbot of Lastingham in Northumberland and was born on that area some time in the early years of the seventh century. This was the area that sprouted such men as the Venerable Bede, St Cuthbert, Wilfrid and Caedmon. Chad and his brother Cedd became Bishops and were pupils of Aiden at Lindisfarne, the Holy Island (in the chapel at Denstone College near Uttoxeter there is a picture of Chad at St Aidan's School). Chad then went to the Celtic heartlands of Ireland and left around the year 654. It is then that fact becomes mixed with conjectures for legends have it that at this point the Holy Man came to Lichfield on his own and became a Hermit, praying in the magic and mystic water that flowed into Stowe Pool and St Chad's Well. His brother Cedd had built the abbey of Lastingham and Chad later took over as Abbot when Cedd died of the yellow fever. Then he became Bishop of York and then Bishop of Winchester. It was when Wulfere, King of Mercia, asked for Chad and other Christian missionaries to help him convert his subjects from their pagan ways to the ways of Christ that the Holy Man was sent to Staffordshire.

Not surprisingly, Chad chose Lichfield as his centre. It was a place that had tremendous religious, cultural and spiritual significance for the entire English race. Those who were not of his faith still looked upon Lichfield as the centre of their beliefs and their hopes and it was the site of the martyrdom of those early Christians. It was also only a stone's throw from two great highways trod by the feet of countless pilgrims over the years and it was only a half day journey away from the Mercian King's homes at Tamworth and Stone.

Here at St Chad's are the remains of the past. A sign by the spot says "The place where thou standest is holy ground". It is ancient indeed.

He became Bishop of Lichfield in the year 669 and today the ancient church of St Chad at Lichfield, in the area called Stowe which means hermitage or holy place, stands upon the site of the saint's cell (when he was a hermit) and St Chad's Well is close by. Interestingly, the earth lines that are so strong in the Lichfield area are at their strongest around St Chad's Church. Does this indicate the true centre of the place was here at St Chad's and that the Cathedral of Lichfield was built at another sacred spot? Some say the Cathedral is over the place where the martyrs fell (and others have it a few miles away).

The well has long been associated with healing waters and pilgrims have flocked to Lichfield for many reasons, personal to themselves. One of the greatest attractions has always been these healing waters but, then again there is much more to draw the pilgrim to this mystical, mythical and magical, middle. Today it does not appear possible to benefit from these waters through inaccessibility. But the area around the well at St Chads is still special. A notice says "The place where thous standest is holy ground".

Festival on the Green Hill

If Lichfield was the place of the dead, then it was almost certainly the place where life triumphed over death as well, for an ancient tradition – its origins lost in the mists of time – is still celebrated to this day and it was a celebration of a floral festival, the time of summer merrymaking and giving thanks for the sun and the flora and crops that rely on the sun. Not a harvest thanksgiving ... that comes later in the year, but a time to thank the Sun God for the life-giving energy.

The centre of this ancient custom, now known as the Lichfield Greenhill Bower Festival or, sometimes, Greenbower Day or Greenbower Gala, was a mound within the confines of Lichfield known as Greenhill. Undoubtedly it was a spot of much significance and was, I feel, a burial mound. It is recorded as being "a place of pagan worship" before a church was constructed there, and it is likely the ancient ceremony dates from then.

In later times this festival came to be associated with the Court of Array and was a military display coupled with the pomp and

157

grandeur of the local dignitaries parading in their finery. It was described in 1817 by a local historian, William Pitt, thus:

"Early on the morning of Whit Monday, the high constables of the city, attended by ten men armed with fire-locks and adorned with ribbons, preceded by eight morris dancers, a clown, fantastically dressed, and drums and fifes, escort the Sheriff, Town Clerk and Bailiffs, from the Guild-hall to the Bower at Greenhill, a mount situated at the south-east extremity of the city in the parish of St Michael, where a temporary booth is erected for their reception. On this mount a title of the court is proclaimed by the common crier; the names of all the householders in the twenty one wards of the city, according as they are enroled, are called over; and all persons owing suit and service to this court, called the Court of Array, or View of Men and Arms of the manor and lordship of Lichfield, are required to appear under pain of a fine and amerciament. After this ceremony is ended the Constables attended by the armed men etc, take their leave and march through the streets to the opposite extremity of the city and summon the Dozener or Petty Constable of that ward, to attend. He immediately comes forth, bearing a flag or ensign, joins the procession and the armed men fire a volley over every house in the ward. The inhabitants on this salute invite the Constables into their houses and present them refreshments, while drink is given to their attendants. The Dozener then, baring his pageant, attends them to the Bower and the Town Clerk from a roll calls forth the name of every householder in the ward. Those who answer to their names are invited into the Booth and regaled with a cold collation and those who neglect to appear are fined one penny each. In this manner the Constables go through the twenty one wards and perform similar ceremonies in each; consequently it is late in the evening before they have performed their toilsome task. The Court of Array is then concluded and the Constables preceded as before by the martial music, dancers and armed men and attended by the Petty Constables formed in two lines, with their gorgeous banners, concludes the festivity by a procession through the principal streets to the Market Place, where on their arrival the Town Clerk in the name of the Bailiffs and Citizens, delivers a charge to the High Constables. The purport of this address is to thank them for their attendance and inform them that in consequence of the firm allegiance of their predecessors several charters and immunities were granted to this city, which it is hoped will stimulate them to the performance of their duty to the King and their fellow citizens. He concludes with advising them to retire peaceably to their homes and pursue the paths of industry and virtue, that they may always be worthy of the peculiar privileges they enjoy as free-born Englishmen, and inhabitants of this loyal and respectful city. The Dozeners then deposit their colours under the belfry in the adjacent church of St Mary."

This was followed by a right old time, with bull baiting, much drinking and a time for the Lords of Misrule to reign. Undoubtedly the pomp and ceremony has taken over from what would have been a feast dedicated to the gods of old at one time.

Today it is interesting to see that a "Green Man" is prominent in the parade. The Wood Spirit, once very alive in Lichfield, is still remembered in this ceremony – perhaps we can, here, find the origins of "Greenhill Bower" ...

The Home of Druid and Hunter

Nestling to the south of the Potteries and snuggling up to Shropshire in the middle of Staffordshire is an area that still clings to the old ways. Travel around Eccleshall and Bishop's Wood and up to Mucklestone, the Mighty Stone of old, and you are in a land that has only begrudgingly joined the present day. It has its roots set firmly in the past and by that I do not mean the recent past. It has an atmosphere of yesterday about it; it is still, thankfully, a place of its own. And long may it be so.

The area to which I allude has as its centre an ancient woodland known as Bishop's Wood. This woodland quarter of Staffordshire, divorced from the ancient hunting grounds of our Norman Kings, is a place that still retains the memories of Druids; it still echoes with traditions of tree worship and it still retains many mysteries that will, perhaps, never be solved. It also retains Earth Magic that can still be savoured.

From the early times of Christianity in these Isles the woodland now known as Bishops Wood was given over to the Church. Of course the area which the forest covered was much greater in those days and was a place to avoid if at all possible. There were few, if any, paths through it. There was game for hunting by the hierarchy and there was the odd hiding place or two for the 'Wolfs' Head', the outcast or the person outside the law, the outlaw. This was a place where tree magic and the legends of the green man, Jack in the Green and the seasonal rituals of life over death and fertility winning the day over infertility was paramount for the inhabitants of the area. And it was a place that the Christians had to dominate in order to eliminate these pagan forms of religion.

These woods were in the ownership of the See of Lichfield and Coventry long before the Norman Conquest. They were known as the Bloor Forest or the Forest of Bloor, or in other versions the Forest of Blore. Most probably there was nothing but a vast tract of trees from over the border in Shropshire around Market Drayton and Newport to the east up to Newcastle under Lyme (where the forest became the Forest of Lyme) in the north and to the south and west as far as Eccleshall. The memory of that name survives at Bloreheath, the site of the massacre of the Lancastrians during the civil War, and at Blore itself, plus Blorepipe near Bishop's Offley. There are many other associations with woodland throughout that area; to name but a few: Wood Farm, Ashfields, Burnt Wood, Shawbroom, Greatwood Farm and Oakley. There are countless more.

Pitt, in his much-quoted "History of Staffordshire" says that when Nero was Emperor of Rome the town of Eccleshall was built on the banks of the River Sowe adjacent to the Forest of Bloor and he adds that the forest was given by Penda, King of Mercia, to the Bishop of Lichfield in 660 AD. It remained in the ownership of the Lichfield See until 1868 and then handed over to the Church Commissioners.

To the north east of what is now Bishop's Wood is the fair hamlet of Fairoak. This is obviously named after one particular tree, the Fair Oak, which meant the Fine Oak or the Great Oak. It was obviously a tree that was special to be chosen out of the many thousands that there would have been in that area and it could have been special because of its age, height or its magic. Or all three. Ancient oaks have, throughout the country, been looked upon as something more than special. It has been associated with many traditions in England, from the time of the Druids who looked upon it as sacred to present day when pilgrims still journey to the ancient oak at Nottingham, known as the Major Oak in Sherwood Forest. The May the 25th celebration of Oak Apple Day may have its roots (no pun intended) in something a lot older that the tradition that Charles II hid in an oak tree just by the Staffordshire border with Shropshire and was subsequently returned to the throne. The traditional merry making used to involve the cutting of oak boughs and decorating houses and churches with them. People would also wear the oak leaf and the oak apple on that day. Up until quite recently this was a tradition kept alive at Uttoxeter, another part of Middle Staffordshire, to the east of the Country. Further north and west in Cheshire there is an oak tree at Marton that was looked upon as a healing tree as well. I discuss this in my book "Cheshire: its Magic and Mystery". And over to the east of Staffordshire at Bagot Park there was long the Beggar's or Bagot's oak tree, a special tree that was venerated over many centuries. And in Needwood Forest, an area where I think the traditions of Robin Hood, the Man in Green, were first brought to life (sorry, Nottingham!) there was the King's Oak and the Swilcar Oak.

Part of Bishop's Wood, in the west of Staffordshire. This spot has been called The Druid's Stone or Holy Stone and is at the head of the Langot Valley.

Just by Fairoak is a spot known as the Langot Valley, and a writer in the early part of the twentieth century, Weston E. Vernon Yonge in "Some Bye-Paths of Staffordshire" for the Staffordshire *Evening Sentinel* thought this had Druidic connections. Mr Yonge, from a very old and renowned local family, wrote that the name Langot had puzzled him. However, he got into conversation with a former vicar of Adbaston, the Rev W. Jackson, who suggested its origins. He said that it was "a reminiscence of the early British and Druids". As in Welsh, and therefore in the old British Language, "Llan" means "holy" and therefore "Llangut" meant "The Holy Stone". This, he conjectured could be taken as meaning the sacred sacrificial stone on the top of some eminence, where High Priests of the Druids celebrated "their blood-stained rites".

Maybe, and maybe not. It could also have meant the Holy Stone that was merely worshipped by the Ancient Britons. Victorian and Edwardian scholars often had a fanciful view of the Ancients. They were, usually, bloodthirsty savages sacrificing people here there and everywhere or they were either Druids like Merlin the Magician or else fur-clad savages. My Yonge was a fine scholar and visionary. He had an immense knowledge and an immense love of the area; but he was tutored in the Victorian times and he, therefore, saw everything with Victorian eyes. But despite this he was able to cast off his blinkers as well and he could then see much more.

He went on to explain that the knoll at the head of the Langot Valley was crowned with trees and at the top is "a sort of table rock". Is this a Druid Stone? he asked. Why not? he replied and explained that for among the oaks of the Bishop's Woods "our savage ancestors might well have raised their temples and offered their human sacrifices".

My Yonge is correct, I feel. There is little or no doubt that this fine wood was once home to the religious activities of the Druids, the wise men of the Celts. The oak tree within their Sacred Groves was very significant to them. Oak and yew, coupled with a stone that emanated energy was their requirement and here that is just what they had.

But before we leave this particular spot amid the woodlands, we must take a look at a hill just above Fairoak and the possible Druid's Stone. It is Goldenhill, and today there is a farm on that spot known, not surprisingly, as Goldenhill Farm – a place, incidentally that used to be owned by people with the surname of Butter! But a Golden Hill was, and is, special. It was the place where the Shining Ones lived or played, the special people ... the fairy folk or the people with the Ancient Knowledge. There are many hills known as "Golden" or "Shining" and this is but one of them, but the origins of its name imply that the hill was looked upon as something special. Perhaps there was a Neolithic burial mound there, this would not be unusual, and people who venerated the Ancients would look upon the spot as still being occupied, or haunted as we say today, by the spirits of the souls of the departed – the Shining Ones.

But more than that, the wood or forest was most definitely home to the woodland traditions, legends and legacies just like the other forests of Staffordshire. It was here that the Green Man traditions abounded, traditions that gave rise to the Puckish embodiment of the impish sprite who took items from some people and gave them to others ... embodied in the tales and traditions of the Spirit of the Green Wood who became the Man in Green, Robin the Hooded Man. He was akin to Herne the Hunter, whose spiritual home is said to be the royal Forest of Windsor. Shakespeare said of him, in "The Merry Wives of Windsor": There is an old tale that goes that Herne the Hunter ... doth all the winter-time, at still midnight, walk round about an oak, with great ragg'd horns – and there he blasts the tree, and takes the cattle, and makes the milch-kine yield blood, and shakes a chain in a most hideous and dreadful manner ... You have heard of such a spirit, and well you know the superstitious idle-headed eld received, and did deliver to our age, this take of Herne the Hunter for truth."

Herne is shown as wearing horns and is associated with the huntsmen of the forests, and has been traced to the Legends of the Wild Hunt that are still alive throughout Europe.

Over to the east of Bishop's Wood, less than half a day's walk, the tradition of the Abbotts Bromley Horn Dance is still very much alive and this could well have its origins in a similar source ... the traditions of the woodlands.

Within two miles of Bishop's Wood is Charnes, known at the time of the Domesday Book as *Cervernestr* from the Latin *Cerve-*

nestris, meaning in English the place or home of the stag. The crest of the Charnes family is a stag's head.

Further north than Bishop's Wood is another wooded area known as the Maer Hills. There is a hill fort there, sometimes called Berth Hill. This is next to War Hill and the spot of two ancient burial mounds. Local tradition has it that the spectres of ancient warriors can often be seen on that hillside. Again, this must have been a special spot. Were the occupants of the ancient graves buried there after they had been killed in battle at War Hill?

There have been ghostly sightings, perhaps not surprisingly, over at blore Heath where the famous Civil War battle was fought and the Lancastrian army was mutilated. At Goldenhills Farm there used to be a breast-plate, a relic from this fight, and there was a cannon ball as well; but a rather strange cannon ball. It was made of a green stone. My mind went back to an interesting but unusual book I once read called *The Green Stone*. It told the story of a group of people who went in search of a mystical green stone in and around this area which, if memory serves me correctly, they discovered. Someone who had a connection with this quest was Andrew Collins, one of this country's leading paranormal investigators and some years later I was to be in regular contact with him concerning earth mysteries in Staffordshire.

A small world. And, before I conclude, perhaps I can make mention of another odd coincidence. I was allowed to look at some very rare photographs that had been in the possession of Sir Philip Brocklehurst at Swythamley Hall. Included among them was a photograph of the Blore Heath Cross (perhaps not surprisingly as his father had been called Philip LANCASTER Brocklehurst) and an old photograph of the Devil's Ring and Finger at nearby Mucklestone. It is those coincidences that make life so much more interesting.

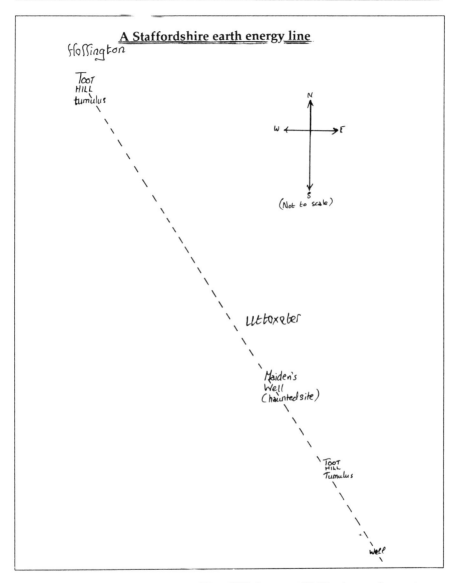

A Staffordshire earth energy line

An energy line connecting two "Toot Hills", one at Hollington and one at
Uttoxeter. Toot or Tewt is dedicated to the god Mercury or could mean
"lookout". There is another Toot Hill at Alton in Staffordshire that overlooks
the site of an ancient battlefield.

9

The Southlands

Black Country Magic: the fires of Baal

At one point, not so very long ago, a continuous fire seemed to rage across the whole of the area of the south of Staffordshire that is known as the Black Country, as the Fires of Baal would have done centuries earlier.

F.W. Hackwood, in his book "Staffordshire Customs, Superstitions, Folklore" (first published 1924 by the Mercury Press and republished in 1974 by EM Publishing Ltd) noticed this and said that in its heyday of iron-trade prosperity "a night view of South Staffordshire, when the sky was lit up by the lurid glare of countless furnaces" looked like Tierra del Fuego, the Land of Fire.

It is difficult today to realise that this tract of land, the victim of the Industrial Revolution and the rape and pillage of natural resources and the landscape, was once a rural idyll where the inhabitants worshipped the Old Gods. But it was not all that long ago. The Industrial Revolution only started some three hundred years ago and before that the land we now, affectionately, call the Black Country because of the soot-stained aspect of its industrial heritage, was as pastoral as any within this Shire. And with it went the ways of the pagans, or the worshippers of the earth.

Fires were lit at the turn of the four seasons and these used to be known as Bale Fires. They marked the progress of the sun in the skies. The Bale Fires are in respect of Bal or Bel, a god of the Celts and of the ancient Hebrews, among others. Fire worship has long been part of the heritage of the human race. By creating fire here on earth we have been able to re-create the all-giving god, known as Sol, the Sun. Or so our predecessors thought.

It had long been the custom throughout these islands and, to a very small degree is still the custom in a few parts of Scotland and Ireland, to light fires on special days and to recreate the sun, especially at the Spring, Summer, Autumn and Winter equinoxes. Most prominent of these fire worship festivals has been that whereby balls of fire have been rolled down hills, Pirehill at Stone may derive its name from this custom. The material engulfed in flames could have been anything from wheat and corn to the carcass of an animal. The fat of animals was often used as a combustible material and coal tar and pitch tar were also often utilised. It is said that the bonfire celebrations, the "good" fires or the bountiful "boon" fires were prevalent in our Black Country area. It has been said that the practice lingered the longest at Wyrley on magic and mysterious Cannock Chase and it is recorded as having occurred at Wednesbury, the town of Woden and at Bilston – the place of Baal.

Bilston, according to Dr Oliver the author of a History of Wolverhampton, derives its name from Beli, one of the principal gods of the old Britons but another writer, Mr W.H. Duignan, wrote: "I know no better etymology of Bilston than the Gaelic 'Beal-tuinn' the fire of Bel, or Baal, the great Gaelic God."

The Beltain Fires were lit all over this land to mark the seasonal passings. They were also known as Bale Fire and the May feast of the Celts was Beltaine or Bealltainn which remembers the old god Beli or Bile. However, others would have it that it is from Bel Tene, "a goodly fire".

The majority of festivals are, or have been, associated with fertility; either the fertility of man and woman, the fertility of their animals or the fertility of their crops. Sometimes these fires of Baal were lit and the cattle and other livestock were passed through them to purify them. Sometimes people were passed through them also for the same purpose. And sometimes people were thrown on them as sacrifices to the god. In some remote parts of the Gaelic world, especially Scotland, a huge effigy of a man was made from straw and wicker. Inside this Wicker Man would be placed sacrifices and they would be set alight. Compare the Wicker Man and our present Guy Fawkes and the connection is easy to find.

There is plenty to remind us that the Black Country was once a green country and was an area alive with the old ways. Between Wolverhampton and Walsall there lies the Manor of Essington. Today, it is a suburban village neighbouring Hilton Park Colliery but, in the past, it has been the centre of an ancient fertility ceremony centred around New Year's Eve, a time of change. This ceremony was carried out at Hilton Hall until the early 1600s when no doubt, the Puritan influences put a stop to the tradition for it involved a brass carved figure known as Jack of Hilton that possessed a huge phallus.

The tenancy of the Hall involved not only payment of annual dues on New Year's Day but also the enactment of an ancient ritual involving this sexually explicit figure. First of all a goose had to be driven around a fire at the Hall three times in a clockwise direction while the fire was being blown with the aid of this figure.

The figure of Jack of Hilton is thought to be of Etruscan origin. It was hollow and depicted a man kneeling on his left knee with a very pronounced phallus covered in what appeared to be oak leaves. During the ceremony water was poured into it and then heated on the fire. When a good head of steam was maintained, the steam would be emitted from the mouth of the figure and, some reports would have it, from the phallus. After this the goose was taken away and cooked, to be eaten by the Lord of the Manor of Essington. The exact meaning of this ritual is obscure. Presumably it ensured fertility for the Lord of the Manor and we are not told if any other form of ritual took place at the same time; the singing of a rhyme or suchlike. The ritual circling of the fire by the goose could be a throw-back to the life-giving fires and the walking, widdershins or clockwise, around an object of worship and there is significance in the number three with Celtic tradition and with later Biblical tradition. It is a tantalising mystery for which a reader may, I hope, be able to provide a solution.

But to return for a moment to Bilston. It has been annexed to the larger township of Wolverhampton for many a year and was once part of the monastery lands given by the Lady Wulfruna who founded Wolverhampton. It is said that it was once just a stockade protecting the wooden hall of the Angle nobleman who founded the place, but perhaps before then it was the area used as a centre of worship to Baal. All around it at one time was a huge expanse of woodland that formed part of the great forest of Cannock and, so wild was this area, that even up until the 1500s the woodland was home to many outlaws. There is a record that in 1509 some robbers entered the old church of St Leonard and stole everything of value. This caused considerable anger and the Bilston folk were granted royal permission to erect a gallows on which these outlaws were to be hanged; but the men of the forest attacked in full force and cut down the gallows. Not content with this they journeyed to Wolverhampton and pulled down the gallows there. This act shows just how many men were taking refuge in the forest at that time; for a force to be able to overcome the defenders of Wolverhampton they must have been great in numbers, or very good fighting men. Perhaps they were both.

This area was part of Mercia, as was the entire County of Staffordshire. Not only was it a part of this ancient kingdom but it was the Royal County. It was the County where the Mercian kings lived and they lived here because it was a natural place for them to be – not only geographically but spiritually as well. Those ancient kings, the descendants of the gods as they were know, had spiritual advisers, descendants of the Bards, Druids and Ovates of the Celtic. These Wise Men or Shaman were the ones who dictated everything to the monarchy of the time; whether it was opportune to go to war, whether it was opportune to marry and where it was opportune to live. How they chose where to live is no mystery; it was a foregone conclusion for many because their predecessors had lived in the same place. They were the benefactors of their fortunes. But originally a place with the right "feel" had to be found, a place that was spiritually uplifting and a place where the monarchs could not only feel at ease but could derive benefit from being there. To some these places were called Holy Places, as Glastonbury, Canterbury, Winchester and Lichfield have been. To others they are the natural place to be where Mother Earth gave off powerful energies. Just go to the spot of their ancient palace or home just outside Stone and see what I mean. Even though it is on private ground and there is no way that the general public can have access to the spot at Bury Bank the entire area still gives off powerful Earth Energies. The Earth Spirit is still alive there.

Worshippers of Woden

When the founders of the Mercian kingdom came to the area we now call the Black Country, probably their first encroachment was at Cannock as well as the northern moorlands and the western

169

borders of Staffordshire. The "English" as opposed to the "British" had a line of advancement that can be traced by their naming of dwelling places, as in Weston, Aston, Walton an Barlaston. These newcomers, later to be known as the English, did not bother to oust all the previous inhabitants and they called the "natives" foreigners. In their tongue this was "The Welsh" which means nothing more than "The foreigners" and the town of Walsall in point of fact derives its name from "Hall or home of the foreigner".

To the west of this area was the boundary of this new kingdom, and we still call it the Marchland today. This march, mark or boundary between Shropshire and Wales was the westerly outpost of this Boundary Land or March Land that became Mercia.

The first monarch of this kingdom known as Mercia was called Crida according to the chronicler Henry of Huntingdon, and as is the case with all societies, their royal leader could claim descent from the gods, just as later monarchs could claim the Divine Right of Kings because of their presumed descent from the Divinity.

Crida, they believed, was descended from Woden. And within this area there were two places of habitation where the residents already worshipped this god: Wednesbury and Wednesfield.

When the town of Wednesbury was founded, the inhabitants obviously worshipped Woden. Woden was the chief god of the Anglo Saxons along with Thunor and Tiw and the goddess Frig. From them we get the names of the days of the week Tuesday, Wednesday and Friday. Wednesbury or Woden's Town is on the confluence of the two head streams of the Tame river. It stands near to the ancient British stronghold of Barr Beacon and would have been fortified, hence the appendage "burh" or fortress.

Did the town grow up around a shrine to Woden or was the town named after its protector, a sort of patron saint, the god Woden? We shall probably never know. Certainly two battles were fought there, one in 591 against the Welsh and another one in 715 between the Mercians and the Men of Wessex and at that time the township was called Woodesbeorg or Wodensbeorge.

Near to Wednesfield there is evidence that this was an area not only known to ancient man but held in reverence as well, because there are at least three lowes or burial mounds: North Lowfield, South Lowfield and Stowman Low.

We have already looked at Wolverhampton in the context of its many healing waters and I think it not an unfair statement that this town owes its original foundation and early growth to these waters. This township looms large over South Staffordshire. There was a monastery at this place for centuries before the Norman invasion and this shows it to have been a spot that was something special. Perhaps the monks came here because there were shrines to the spirits of the water, who knows. This town is set on a high place, itself a clue to the sanctity of the area for most ancient sites are on high ground. Most churches named after St Michael or St George are on these places of the dragon where good overcame evil, the church overcoming paganism, the saints defeating the dragons. But in this case the church is dedicated to St Peter. It stands on a 500 feet high mound and the very name Wolverhampton means Wulfrun's Heantown or High Town. It was Lady Wulfrun, sister of King Edgar, who gave much land and money to the collegiate church in 994. But why did she do this, or to be more blunt, what was in it for her?

There was, of course, much royal patronage of monasteries and churches and had been since Christian, and indeed pre-Christian, times. Paying dues on earth was always a sure way of buying a place in heaven, or so it was thought by those ancestors of ours. In those times it was not only action and deed but also the size of the purse that was believed to be the key to heaven.

The good lady used to come to the area to bathe in healing waters later known as Wulfruna's Well and also known as Lady Wulfruna's Spring. It was also known as Spring Vale and much later became the site of a steel works.

It is recorded that these waters were "much sought after by the sick and suffering" and with the royal patronage of Wulfruna would have been very popular indeed.

I wonder whether this religious site was placed there because of the proximity to these healing waters. Had it been a site of significance before this monastery or collegiate church was founded there, I wonder? Perhaps at one time a Hermit or Anchorite stood lone vigil over these beneficial waters and this holy man was, perhaps, on the spot where pagan people had benefited from the waters.

171

Houses cut into rock at Kinver Edge on the southern border of Staffordshire. Kinver Edge has been a site special to man for many centuries and there is still evidence of pre-Christian worship at this spot.

Wolfbaines of the Chase

What a magical and mystical place is Cannock Chase and the region around. Once an area full of giant oak trees, the home of the Celtic Holy Men and home to the stag and the wild boar, the wolf and the fox; it later became the happy hunting grounds of nobility. It has also been the home of many an outlaw and, while much of its legend and tradition has been eaten away just like its trees, it retains many memories of that which has gone before.

Undoubtedly this area was known to our ancient forebears for the area has a number of tumuli within it. There is an interesting ancient burial place close by Milford and surrounded by three hills. It is a cup-shaped mound known locally as The Bury and when this was excavated there were three sets of human bones all consumed by fire. Were they cremated before being buried? Perhaps, but it seems to be a case of rather over-egging the pudding to cremate then to bury in a large mound. Perhaps they were all sacrificial victims ... victims of the Fires of Baal, perhaps? There is a local tradition that this is the burial place of three kings, or leaders of tribes, who were slain in battle and it is worth noting that this tradition was in evidence before the excavations discovered there to be three bodies. Perhaps they were divine victims ... rulers who had to suffer the fate of the Divine King and be ritually killed by their subjects after a certain length of time. Whatever the reason, they have been there for a great length of time and are testimony to the fact that parts of the Chase were looked upon as holy.

With so much of the woodland having gone either through natural devastation or man-made devastation, it is of no surprise that today there is very little evidence of Celtic occupation but the area would have had Celtic holy men there, it is almost certain. The clues are most definitely still around.

The township of Cannock itself has been described as breathing the atmosphere of coal mines. Its people are among the friendliest in Staffordshire. And that, make no mistake about it, is praise indeed. The Chase itself stretches for many miles north and east and is now an expanse of high moorland. Its southern area is pock-marked with coal-mines but, where once thousands of oaks grew, there is now a vast expanse of heathland. Conifers standing to attention like rows of troops on parade have been planted and there are many silver birches, but where, oh where are the oaks in any great number?

In its northern region of old, to the east of Acton Trussell and immediately south of Brocton, there is in all probability a remnant of the old religion when, as we have discussed, the Fires of Baal were lit and blazing wheels of fire were hurled down hills. For just above the spring known as Oldacre Burn is a hill known as Tar

Hill. Is this name a remnant of the days when burning tar was used to appease the Beltaine god? Just south south west of here is a farm that is called Belt View Farm and again I must ask if this has connections with the Beltaine Fires.

Huntington is to the south of here, and I have often wondered whether this name owes anything to Robin Hood, Earl of Huntingdon. We all know that the Nottinghamshire "poachers" have taken our man in green from us but back in the days when forest covered most of this country the Forest of Needwood, said to be the birthplace of Robin of Loxley and Earl of Huntingdon was a continuation of the Forest of Cannock. Are Huntington and Huntingdon one and the same?

Graves at St Michael's, Penkridge. Hilary and I were drawn to this spot and she saw the ghost of a little girl dashing in and out of the headstones. She wore a white dress with ruffled sleeves. One of the graves was of a five year old named Sarah Elizabeth, we discovered afterwards.

Further to the west and now geographically out of what is known as "The Chase" is Penkridge. This was once a Roman settlement just by Watling Street, a road used by the Romans but a line of communication, no doubt, before they reached these shores. Before the Roman influence on Penkridge this place was an important Celtic place of worship; undoubtedly a Sacred Grove in the midst of the dense oak forest. The name of this village or township means a small ridge and in Roman days it was called Pennocrucium which, according to Anne Ross and Don Robins in their excellent work "The Life and Death of a Druid Prince" (published by Rider, 1989) is from the Celtic meaning "head of the mound" or "chief mound". As there is no hill around they both think the name implies an assembly-place centred upon a grave mound. In their book they have discovered that Penkridge links the sacrificial site in Cheshire at Lindow Moss where the bog man was found in the late 1980s with the battleground of Mancetter. I recommend their book to you to follow these threads.

They add that Pennocrucion is the same as the Gaelic god of the Irish harvest, Cenn Croich who is also known as Crom Dubh, the Dark One and this may associate Penkridge with the worship of this "fearsome deity" – The Dark One.

Travel further westward across from The Chase and away from Penkridge and then Beacon Hill comes into view, perhaps just what it implies, a place where the warning and communicating beacons were shone to give messages across the land; or perhaps it was a place where a beacon fire was lit to guide the traveller or the hunter across this tract of land. The most sensible way across and through the expanse of The Chase would always have been via Watling Street, but there would have been many reasons why travellers would have chosen other routes. Then again, perhaps the beacon was purely for the huntsman.

Near to the tiny hamlet of Lapley beyond Beacon Hill there are the remains of a hermitage or cell. I would ask you, once again, to try to envisage how lonely a place this area would once have been; thousands of trees competing for space and few if any tracks through them. There in the middle of this huge wooded area was where a holy man chose to be alone, save for the pilgrims who would visit for healing of the body, the mind or the soul. A Benedictine Priory was founded here in the eleventh century but there is little or nothing left of it today, save for a few bits of stonework. The church itself is still standing but its transepts have gone. Nevertheless, it has been described as an awe-inspiring building.

Continue westward and further out of The Chase and the traveller comes to another tiny hamlet, this time Blymhill, pronounced "Blimmil", on the Shropshire borders. This is an interesting spot full of earth mystery to this day. Just north there is Holywell Plantation, but a holy well could not be found. Travel north from here and we come to Osslow, its name denoting an ancient burial lowe.

But back to The Chase. It was the Normans who were the great hunters in their Royal Forests but long before these Frenchmen came to England the Bishops of Lichfield kept Cannock Chase as their own hunting spot. For these good and holy men thrilled to the chase and the hunt and it was only after the Conquest that they were denied the rights of the hunt on these lands. However, Richard the 1st, the Lionheart, while raising money for the Third Crusade, sold the Rugely and Cannock manorial rights and their forest rights to the Bishop of Lichfield, Hugh de Novan. This part of the forest became known as The Bishop's Chase and later the whole of the district took on the title of The Chase.

This, like all the other hunting forests, was vigorously defended. It was quite all right for the King, the Bishop and their guests to kill whatever they fancied for the sport. Should anyone else kill or attempt to kill an animal within the confines of The Chase then the punishment was severe. If a small animal was taken such as a rabbit or perhaps a polecat, then the punishment was the loss of an eye or a limb. But to stray beyond those sizes and take a deer then the poacher's life would be taken by the Foresters, the people appointed to preserve the Forest for the regal owners.

Of course, poaching went on but because the punishment was so severe, the persons who had, perhaps, killed a deer would go to extreme lengths not to be caught. And perhaps the safest way was, perversely, to go into the forest to hide. Many did this and banded together to form groups of outlaws, known as Wolfbains. These were the stuff of Robin Hood and His Merry Men and their way of life within the woods spawned many a tradition of woodland lore as we have seen before.

Lady Godiva rides again

Before we conclude our perambulations and our search for the magical and the mysterious, we must make mention of the legendary Lady Godiva. "Legendary" may be but she was, of course, a real flesh and blood person, as "Peeping Tom" could no doubt testify. This eleventh century wife of the Mercian Earl Leofric is, of course, famous for her ride through the streets of Coventry clad only in her birthday suit and astride a white horse. But there is more to her than that, and she is essential to our investigations of the Black Country for this tale contains only half truths and echoes of pre-Christian cults.

To the south west of Wolverhampton is the area known as Penn and it has a very interesting church, situated just off the main A449 road. Against the southern wall of this church, on the outside, is the base of a cross that was known as the Godiva Cross. This base was unearthed in 1912 and it is now thought that it was perhaps buried when the current church was built. In with the new, out with the old, as it were. An inscription says that the cross (of which there is now no trace) was erected by Godiva, Lady of the Manor of Nether Penn and the wife of the Earl of Mercia, Leofric. It also says that itinerant priests were provided by Dudley Priory to take occasional services up until the present church (or, at least, its shell) was built by Sir Hugh de Bushbury round about 1200.

So what of this Lady of the Manor and her ride through Coventry? Of course Coventry does not feature in this book about magical and mysterious Staffordshire but she was the wife of the Earl who owned the entire Shire and so is worthy of mention ... especially when it gives an inclination as to the religious actions and the hidden, pagan thoughts, of the people she ruled over.

For this insight I am indebted to a man from Somerset, no less, by the name of Paul Newman. He wrote an immensely interesting book called "Gods and Graven Images" which in the main deals with the chalk figures of the southern regions. It was published by Robert Hale in 1987.

Within this book there is a fascinating chapter titled "Mighty Queens and Sacred Stallions" and he recounts Godiva's legendary ride through the streets of Coventry. He quotes the rhyme "Ride a cock horse to Banbury Cross, see a fine lady upon a white horse: rings on her fingers, bells on her toes, and she shall have music wherever she goes".

There is a suggestion that this "fine lady", who was named Celia

Fiennes, was a descendant of a female fertility figure. The rings and bells could have been used to frighten away evil spirits just as church bells were used to summon the good and send away the evil.

He recounts the legend of Godiva riding, naked, through the streets of Coventry because she had interceded when he was taxing the citizens too highly and he said he would grant her request if she rode through the streets of Coventry unclad. He also refers to the Peeping Tom legend who was struck blind for peeping at the Lady and he recalls by this the punishment given to Actaen who saw Diana, the moon goddess, in her naked glory. He says that, therefore, the figure of Godiva is older than implied and the wife and her husband are figures in an ancient symbolic pageant bringing forward the ancient horse ceremonies whereby a real or a symbolic naked victim was given to the Earth Mother.

This ceremony is an echo of Celtic tradition. The white horse has featured greatly in Celtic myth and is but one more example of how the people of Staffordshire have their traditions enshrouded by the mists of time: a ghost on Butterton Moor rides a white horse, for instance.

The way ahead

Staffordshire is a proud county comprising proud people. It is also a very ancient shire, and one that is not appreciated by the vast majority of people for what it is. It is a place of much beauty and it is a place of much magic. Far too much of its magic is hidden, and that is why (I now know) my old Aunt told me that this was the Hidden County.

How right she was. There is still much mystery to uncover within this wonderful land; perhaps one day we shall journey together again to unravel some more. Until then I hope I have perhaps encouraged you to investigate this place. As I have said, scratch the surface and the veneer will shine through.

Magic is within its soil, the Earth Spirit is still within its stones and much that has gone before is still floating in its mists.

Good hunting.

The church at Wychnor (sometimes spelt Wichnor) with its Elizabethan tower.
This is the tiny hamlet that boasted the "Wychnor Flytch" a piece of bacon that
was awarded to a couple who had never had a cross word for a year and a day
... a wooden carved piece of bacon used to be over the fireplace at the great
hall, now a country club and hotel. The area has also a legend of a ghost.

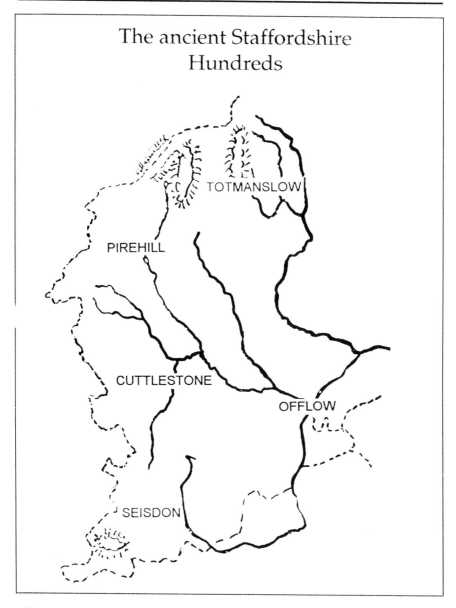

The ancient Staffordshire Hundreds

The old areas of the County. Totmanslow denotes a burial place; Pirehill could have been a site of fires, probably to Baal (the Beltaine Fires) and Offlow could refer to the burial site of Offa, who built the famous Dyke.

Index